Andrea and Markus Eschbach

Riding Free

Bitless, Bridleless, Bareback

Translated by Julia Welling

TRAFALGAR SQUARE
North Pomfret, Vermont

First published in 2011 by
Trafalgar Square Books
North Pomfret, Vermont 05053

Printed in China

Originally published in the German language as *Reiten so frei wie möglich* by Franckh-Kosmos Verlags-GmbH & Co. KG, Stuttgart

Disclaimer of Liability
The authors and publisher shall have neither liability nor responsibility to any person or entity with respect to any loss or damage caused or alleged to be caused directly or indirectly by the information contained in this book. While the book is as accurate as the authors can make it, there may be errors, omissions, and inaccuracies.

Trafalgar Square Books encourages the use of approved safety helmets in all equestrian sports.

Library of Congress Cataloging-in-Publication Data
Eschbach, Andrea, 1971-
 [Reiten so frei wie möglich. English]
 Riding free : bitless, bridleless or bareback / Andrea Eschbach, Markus Eschbach.
    p. cm.
 Includes index.
 Summary: "A how-to guide for horseback riders who wish to ride their equine partners with minimal tack and equipment. Teaches riders how to safely control their mount without a bit, bridle, or saddle"-- Provided by publisher.
 ISBN 978-1-57076-484-4 (pbk.)
 1. Horsemanship. I. Eschbach, Markus, 1968- II. Title.
 SF309.E8313 2011
 798.2--dc23
                    2011031688

All photographs by Christiane Slawik/Kosmos *except*: pp. 23–8, 36, 38, 42–3, 46–8, 51, 97–101 (Gudrun Braun); pp. 22, 29, 45 *bottom*, 102, 104 (Peter Kindler)

Illustrations by Robert Cook

Cover design by RM Didier
Typefaces: Proforma, Strada, Strada Condensed

10 9 8 7 6 5 4 3 2 1

Contents

In many of the pictures in this book, authors Andrea and Markus Eschbach are not wearing riding helmets. They are, however, aware of the significance of being role models and explicitly advise you to wear a helmet complying with current safety standards whenever riding a horse.

Preface

"You should write a book!"

Even though people frequently suggested the idea, we never dreamed of becoming book authors ourselves—that is, until recently. Our active life as

horse trainers and clinicians kept us so busy that we could not imagine having the time and energy to write a book. As you can see, we somehow managed!

Again and again, we have been surprised by the increasing demand for the techniques we teach—considering the fact that they are nothing new. We haven't reinvented the wheel, nor are we hiding the Holy Grail in our barn.

We also have to admit that, like anyone else, we constantly wonder whether we are doing the "right thing." Our four-legged friends keep reassuring us that we are. Unaffected by the media, the Internet, and current fads and trends, they send us completely honest signals that say: "Keep going! What you are doing is all right!"

Our students can be divided into different categories:

> There are the beginning riders who take a critical look at different clinicians and their techniques, then use common sense to evaluate them, and who do not feel like paying someone to put them down and make them feel bad.

> Then there are those who already know a lot about riding and horses but still feel the need to discover something new—and those who have tried it all and still cannot get ahead.

> Finally, there are the horse owners who can self-reflectively say to themselves, "My horse has a problem with me."

The people who come to us are curious, timid, shy, enthusiastic, confused, intense, resigned, interested, happy, searching, doubtful, questioning, and creative...to name just a few characteristics! It is a mystery to us why so many essentially very different people come to us and want to learn something. But what we do know for sure is that nobody leaves us indifferent.

It might be because people are finding themselves in the process?

Andrea and Markus Eschbach

Look at Fabiola (p. v) and Smiley (this page) and consider their expression. It is amazing to see how "freedom" positively affects the emotional state of horses.

Freedom is defined as an absence of necessity, coercion, or constraint in choice or action. As riders, we can decide how we want to train and ride our horses. Our goal must be to do this in a way that makes our horses want to work for and with us.

Much of what you will read in this book you may already know. Why should you take the time and study it anyway? Because we want confident readers and confident riders—confident in thinking, dreaming, and feeling.

We developed our techniques according to the rules and methods established by our horses; in other words, our work is based on what we know about natural equine behavior. Our first approach toward horses is always from the ground: Groundwork builds the foundation that allows us to ride without restraints.

Groundwork— What's the Point?

Thorough groundwork, developed step by step, is a fundamental building block of our method. We think it is safe to say that, essentially, good riding depends on it. You will find it much easier to transfer techniques to horseback when you have learned to master them on the ground first. We are not talking about specific "exercises" per se, but instead about every aspect of riding your horse needs to know in order to be a proper "riding horse." Groundwork is a great way to prepare, practice, and school these techniques.

When you start training a young horse, groundwork allows you to explain to him fundamental aspects of his equine education. Without having to bear your weight, your horse can concentrate on your careful and detailed instructions. This is helpful because often, horses do not do as we wish because they simply do not understand what we want. Even though your ultimate goal might be to familiarize your horse with the reins, bridle, and bit in order to prepare him for riding, you cannot expect him to automatically know exactly what they mean and what he should do with them.

You have the responsibility to make your horse understand what you want by explaining your objectives step by step and without scaring or intimidating him. Returning to our example of familiarizing the horse to the bit and bridle, for example, you need to get him used to being touched on his head and inside his mouth—as these areas are very sensitive—before you introduce the tack.

People often do not take the time to thoroughly explain riding techniques to their horses. Others do not understand how horses learn and so don't know how to convey their intentions. What we want is for our horses to react to anything we do with automatic, or even reflexive, "positive" habits, so we must prepare them properly.

What Do We Expect from Our Horse?

A good riding horse is not only expected to be great under saddle but also to be easily handled and controlled from

We think it is very important to proceed in a methodical and step-by-step manner when schooling young horses. Based on this principle, when preparing a horse for the bit (if doing so is necessary), we start by familiarizing the horse with touches on the corners of his mouth, his tongue, and gums before moving on.

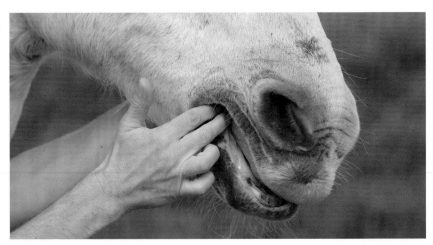

Gentle strokes applied to the gums have a calming effect on the horse. We use a form of TTouch from the Tellington Method® developed by Linda Tellington-Jones (see *The Ultimate Horse Behavior and Training Book* for detailed instructions—www.horseandriderbooks.com). Such stroking affects the brain's limbic system, which is in charge of emotions.

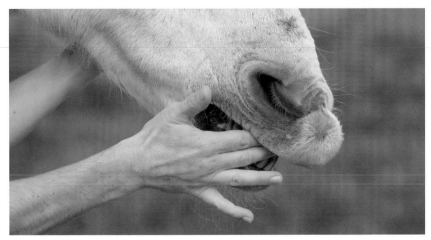

the ground. The energy or force we must use when working with him (whether on the ground or in the saddle) should always be minimal.

We also expect our horse to be attentive. This is not to say, of course, that we want him trained to stare at us constantly and without blinking! We simply want him to react to the slightest requests (in the form of, for example, a quiet cluck of the tongue, slight weight shifts, or changes in hand position) by turning toward us and waiting for what we have to say.

Naturally, we would like our horse to show a certain amount of interest in and curiosity about the things we say and do. Curiosity is a great motivator to get a horse to become your teammate and to work with you. In the same way, we have the responsibility to create training sessions our horse finds interesting and that make him want to

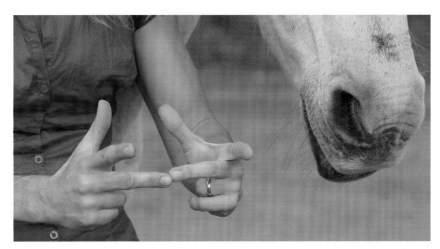

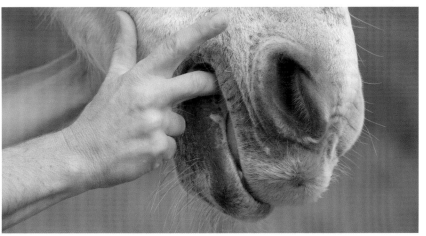

Another step toward familiarizing your horse with a bit: Insert one middle finger into your horse's mouth by sliding it through the gap between his front and back teeth. Then, on the other side of his mouth, insert your other middle finger. Rest both middle fingers on your horse's tongue. Proceed gently and carefully!

When you do put on a
bridle, you should do so
without forcing your
horse's head into a
specific position. Your
horse should willingly
cooperate (that is, lower
his head).

work for us. This requires creativity on our part: Diversion and a great degree of variability are the keys to success. However, you must be sure you do not lose focus or sight of your actual training goal.

We work all our horses alternately on the ground and under saddle. This includes rope work, round pen training, going for walks in-hand, ponying, longeing, long reining, and trainer Michael Geitner's "Dual Activation" (he uses dual colored poles—blue and yellow—to activate both sides of the horse's brain while training the horse to navigate obstacles). While we have both beginner and advanced students ride our horses, we always make sure to maintain and advance the horses' training level ourselves. We do a lot of trail rides, under saddle or bareback, wearing different forms of (bitless) bridles or a neck ring (see p. 76).

It is important to note, however, that we do not simply do whatever our horses feel like doing at any given time. We always want to be the ones leading each training session, but we strive to do so consistently and while allowing for a constant dialog with and empathetic observation of our student—the horse.

A skillful and smart instructor produces students who love to learn. That is our personal goal when training horses.

The "Talk" before the "Talk"

The first moment of contact between you and your horse takes place when the two of you become aware of each other's presence for the first time.

The horse's perception is much more acute than that of human beings. Therefore, we can conclude that a horse will, in all likelihood, register our arrival long before we actually see him.

Because of this, a form of relationship or "contact" is established long before we start actually working with our horse in the ring or round pen. So with this in mind, when you walk down the barn aisle toward your horse's stall, you should already be consciously aware of what exactly it is you want to do with your equine partner. Since you are meeting your horse to take him out for "work," your thoughts should be focused exclusively on him. For example, imagine your horse standing in his stall, with his ears pricked and an expectant expression on his face, as you make your way toward him. Of course, this does not necessarily mean that your horse will actually look that way when you reach him! This form of mental exercise is simply supposed to heighten your senses and your perception, and leave you better prepared to respond to your horse even before the first moment of physical contact.

The next step in establishing contact with your horse occurs in the moment the two of you actually see each other. We often talk about "first impressions" in human interaction—during the initial seconds of an encounter, our senses register important details that can possibly determine the future of a relationship. This applies to horses, as well. Approaching a first impression with acute awareness and receptive sensors, we might just gain some important information about our horse that could help us better assess him.

Be conscious of every move and step you make. Taking our horse out of his stall, for example, is usually just a means to an end that we do not think much about. Our mind is already someplace else, which significantly restricts our perception. Our horse, on the other hand, notices exactly what our state of mind is like and how attentive we are being. When we are careless, even in something as casual as leading a horse from his stall, we often give away valuable "points" with which our horse rates our behavior. We do not even realize it, but we may have just left a first impression of being careless. Our future credibility, in our horse's eyes, is tied to these first moments.

Horses are highly sensitive and recognize immediately what kind of mood we are in. Therefore, make sure that you put all "negative" thoughts aside when you are on your way to greet your horse, well before you actually reach him.

Teaching the horse to lower his head on cue: Use two fingers to apply slight pressure to the poll; this tells the horse that he is supposed to lower his head.

Coming Up with a "Central Theme"

Countless times, we have met riders at our clinics who, when working with or riding their horse, have no concrete plan for the session or even a clear idea

Info   Be Mentally Collected

Before we even greet our horse for the first time, we can influence the way in which the day's training session will proceed. Understand the importance of maintaining a heightened awareness focused on your horse—even before you can actually see him. Practice your ability to "center your thoughts" or "collect" yourself mentally before enter the barn each day.

of what they are actually "working" on. They do not have a picture in their mind of what exactly they want to achieve and how they might get there.

Very few riders are able to give a precise estimate when asked about how long they are planning on working with their horse on a given day. In some cases, their "planning" does not cover more than what will amount to the next 10 seconds! We must, therefore, conclude that many riders simply work on whatever, wherever, and with whichever technique comes to mind—however long they are on their horse's back or at his side.

Based on this fact alone, how are horses supposed to deliver the clear and precise results we expect of them? How are they supposed to find the motivation to work with us if they never

exactly know how long a training session is going to take and therefore how to best conserve and/or use their energy? Why should they want to learn from us if they find that they often have to keep working even when they are exhausted or cannot concentrate? Does it surprise you that these horses do not enjoy working?

In this book, we want to give you clear advice on how to prepare your horse and ride him with as little tack and/or equipment as possible. We will begin with establishing contact and control at the horse's head. Returning once more to our bridle example, you familiarize your horse to the sensation of being touched around and in the mouth, and to tolerate a foreign object (your fingers—see p. 3) inside his mouth. Even if you are not planning on

Tip Lowering the Head

Teaching your horse to lower his head on cue from the ground is a fundamental exercise, especially when you consider the frame he is supposed to move in under saddle. Having the ability to lower your horse's head at any time also contributes to safety. When a horse is scared and feels threatened, his head will reflexively shoot up into the air as his body prepares for flight or fight. When you can get your horse to lower his head immediately so that he assumes a relaxed posture, you might just "snap him out of it." In this way, you can refocus the horse's attention on you and better control the situation. Lowering the head gives you a chance to actively influence the learning ability and general suppleness of your horse.

When your horse shows the desired reaction and lowers his head, the pressure on his poll has to immediately stop and your hand must be removed.

using a bit, it is helpful for your horse to be familiar with having things put in his mouth—especially when it comes to dental work, medication, and de-worming. By building a foundation in a stress-free manner and getting your horse used to things like the bit, should you change your mind later on and de-cide to use a bit after all, your horse will be well prepared for the transition.

Yielding

Flexing

As early as the groundwork stage, your horse should learn to gently and will-ingly yield to the slightest cue to flex laterally and immediately follow even the smallest degree of pull whether to the left or the right. (Note: Flexing and bending should first be practiced with a halter. Only when your horse has learned to gently yield to a halter should you transition to a bridle with reins.) When your horse yields (even just a little bit), it is important to imme-diately suspend pressure and reward him for his behavior.

In the top two pictures on this page, Andrea is showing her mare what she means by "flexing in the poll" (lateral-ly). With her right hand, Andrea mas-sages the mare's neck behind the poll and uses the left rein to signal her to yield and flex her head to the left. The movement Andrea asks for is very small.

Bending

In the same way as flexing laterally in the poll, we can use groundwork to im-prove our horse's compliancy and later-al flexibility in other areas of neck and head. This helps your horse become more supple and prepares him for lat-

eral rein aids. It also builds the foundation for directing and controlling your horse's forehand, which is necessary if you want to ride him.

In order to bend her mare, in the photo on the lower left Andrea places her palm flat on the horse's shoulder and uses the left rein to bend the neck, which should bend sideways in an even arc.

Using Reins for Bending

After her mare has learned to flex and bend while Andrea is standing next to her head (first with a halter and lead, and then with a bridle and reins), Andrea assumes a position back along the horse's barrel, next to where the saddle is placed. Andrea then asks the horse to flex and bend, using the reins to aid as she would when sitting in the saddle.

Forward-Downward

In several individual steps, we explain to the horse how to stretch his neck forward-downward, beginning on the ground (see photos on this page). Again,

when your horse has learned to lower his head in response to the slightest amount of pressure applied to his poll (see p. 6), you can proceed to asking him with the reins. Practice at a halt before doing the same exercise at a walk and trot.

Sideways-Downward

If your horse tends to carry his head high, he will most likely exhibit lateral stiffness: In this case, a combined exercise during which your horse has to yield sideways and down at the same time is very useful (see bottom photo, this page). It is simply a combination of bending and forward-downward, both of which you have already practiced.

You are discovering one of our basic principles: "The art of small steps." Learn to master basic skills and think of them as tiny building blocks you have to put together to form a whole.

Different Groundwork Techniques

Our approach divides groundwork into the following sections:
> Round pen: Free round penning that emphasizes precise observation and "reading" of the horse; interpreting his signals and using them to establish better communication.
> Lead rope: "Leading" in our program implies both "being led" and "complying/following"; working on different leading positions.
> Rope work: Working with a rope halter and lead rope, and learning to yield to direct and indirect contact.
> Safety training: "Anti-spook" training and trail exercises, including playfully mastering a groundwork trail course.

Most horses find it easier to stretch and yield downward when their neck is flexed or bent to the side. In this position, the muscles on one side of the neck are already relaxed, and vertical and lateral flexion are united.

With this mare, Andrea established vertical and lateral flexion separately before putting it together like pieces of a puzzle. As mentioned earlier, it is very important that you yield immediately to reward your horse and confirm that he reacted to your cue in the right way. This is how your horse learns what you want.

> Work in hand: Exercises with both halter and bridle to introduce the aids, as well as take the first steps toward being able to do arena figures (serpentines, circles, and the like).

> Work on the long reins: We consider this stress-free "riding from the ground"; through the use of two longe lines, we can efficiently gymnasticize the horse while liberating him from the traditional longeing circle.

> Dual Activation: This balanced and gentle form of training created by Michael Geitner activates both cerebral hemispheres in the horse's brain, training coordinated motion and balance in an effective and quick manner. Your horse will gain mental equanimity and confidence in his physical abilities. He builds up his muscles physiologically so improving performance takes less energy.

> Our groundwork program also includes elements of the Tellington Method, developed by Linda Tellington-Jones, and is further influenced by therapeutic work (physical therapy).

(Photos on p. 10)
To teach her mare to stretch forward-downward, Andrea places the right rein over the horse's neck and holds the left rein in a way that brings both her hands close to each other. With the right rein, Andrea signals her mare to lower her head. She immediately yields when the horse reacts correctly. To lead the mare's head even lower toward the ground, Andrea crouches next to her.

Today, a wide range of bitless bridles are available to the consumer, and an increasing number of riders are interested in this form of equipment. This chapter is going to teach you how to prepare yourself and your horse, step by step, so that riding with a bitless bridle becomes efficient, harmonious, and safe.

Many Riders—One Way?
Many Riders—Many Ways!

On the pages that follow we'll show you ways to ride and control horses in a correct and gentle manner using a bitless bridle. With so many options now available, the sensible place to start is by deciding which bridle suits your horse best. Opinions differ with regard to this question. Which bridle is "right"? Which bridle is the best? Which criteria should you base your choice on?

Making a Decision

You may be wondering whether to use a regular (with a bit) or a bitless bridle on your horse. That is a good start. Things like the saddle pad and saddle, breast collar and bridle, we usually just pick up and put on our horse without giving them much thought since they are considered the "basic equipment" necessary for riding.

We were no exception in this regard since we started riding many years ago, and in the same way as you probably did. We just did what our instructor told us. We had not thought about requisite

We ride our horses with bitless bridles, both with and without a saddle. For safety reasons, we advise you to always wear a riding helmet.

tack and equipment or learned to ask questions about what may or may not be necessary. Only many years later did we start taking a closer, more critical look, and at that time we began searching for different forms of bridles that might offer the horse more freedom.

And this is where we want to begin: We want our students (and our readers) to start thinking for themselves. We want to inspire curious, inquisitive riders who ask questions, come up with their own ideas, and show enough courage to look at things from a different perspective.

Why Do We Use Bridles?

The most common form of regular bridle used for beginner riders is a simple snaffle. The bit inside the horse's mouth is used for communication, steering, control, and refinement of the aids.

Since we use our hands as our most important tools, they are the most well-developed and trained human appendage. Consequently, our hands (by way of the reins) have the greatest power over the horse. Of course, communicating with the horse does not only mean using the reins but should be a harmonious interplay of all forms of aids (seat and legs, for example). Nevertheless, your hands are capable of exerting pressure on and manipulating the horse's head via the reins.

This is where we meet the most severe problems in riding: Rough, insensitive hands (by way of reins and bit) quickly destroy the delicate contact we wish to use for communication with the horse. The inventors of bits are very creative. They keep building ever more ingenious, mechanical instruments, which promise new advantages for the rider, supported by state-of-the-art tests and research. Your potential choice of

bits and bridles is huge and manufacturers want you to believe that for every difficult situation, there is a matching bridle you can use to magically solve the problem. Depending on the kind of bit, the effect is strongest on the horse's tongue, bars, or palate. Where is this progression headed?

Unfortunately, reality is never that easy and straightforward. Otherwise, the number of problems riders commonly encounter with their horses would be much fewer—considering the sheer number of "tools" available!

Info "Experts"

Particularly complex and/or potentially harsh bits and training aids belong only in the hands of an expert. This is a sentence we often hear, and yet isn't it a contradiction in terms? Should not an expert require much less mechanical assistance to produce even greater results?

There are bits out there that, quite simply, belong in the medieval section of a museum under the heading "instruments of torture." They neither belong in the mouth of a horse nor in the hands of a rider. The inventors of bits are fully aware of the mechanical effects and the resulting discomfort they create in the mouth of the horse. But what we find particularly interesting is that the product information that accompanies the bit on packaging or in catalogs often says things like "prevents rearing" or "keeps tongue in place," but exactly how the bit works is hardly ever explained. It is extremely alarming that users (riders) usually do not have the faintest idea of the effect the bit they are using has on their horse's mouth.

While warning readers against

A small sampling of some of the bitless bridles available:

1: Lindell, a form of side pull created by Linda Tellington-Jones (www.ttouch.com).
2: Rope halter, perfect for groundwork, with rings worked into the halter to allow you to attach reins to use for riding.
3: Side pull.
4: Simple leather bosal.
5: Hackamore.

Left: Unfortunately, many Spanish horses are marked by a scar like this one—a reminder of years of being ridden with a "Serreta," a serrated metal nosepiece very popular in Spain.

Right: The Bitless Bridle™ developed by Robert Cook (www. bitlessbridle.com). The noseband is supposed to rest between 1½ and 2 inches above the corners of the horse's mouth.

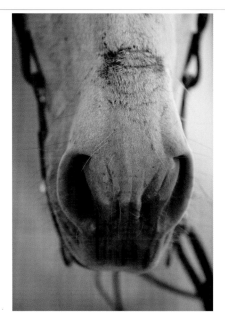

sharp bits, we must not forget that in the wide world of bridles, there can also be found other "instruments" that should be locked away and forgotten as quickly as possible. For example, there are those that feature metallic parts in places where the bridle puts direct and concentrated pressure on the nose or other parts of the horse's head. We lived and worked in Spain for 10 years and are very familiar with the usual "marks" of pain left by the Serreta (the common serrated metal nosepiece) and other features like it. Almost all of our own horses that were imported from Spain have scars from this device.

The Peruvian bosal can also be harmful when the noseband is fastened too tightly and placed so low as to rest on the part of the horse's nose that is cartilage. Injuries and breathing problems are the result. Sharp mechanical hackamores are just as questionable.

In the end we can conclude: The fact that a bridle does not have a bit does not necessarily make it more horse-friendly. In addition, harmful bridles or those causing pain do not belong anywhere

near a horse. In the end, it makes no difference if you harm your four-legged partner on purpose or by mistake—pain is pain. We strongly disapprove of equipment designed to cause great discomfort (or pain) or that deliberately uses pain to give a handler control. Our opinion is not only based on ethical reasons, but on the fact that such equipment is pointless if your objective is to train your horse. Horses do not learn well, if at all, when under stress.

In flight animals such as the horse, tolerance for pain and/or perceived threat is usually very low—even slight pain might trigger a flight response. And even if the horse does not resort to flight right away, he will definitely show signs of retreat and resistance. He will look for protection—both mental and physical. These reflexive behavior-

Info | Pain-Free Learning

Trying to train horses when using pain and discomfort as a motivator is pointless as horses cannot learn when under stress.

al patterns safeguarded the horse's survival in the wild. It is ingrained: If possible, withdraw from life-threatening situations by running away. If flight is impossible, start to fight!

Naturally, we do not want to trigger flight or fight responses in our horse as this would pose a massive safety risk to us and to our horse. Paradoxically, some riders do not seem to know anything about natural horse behavior or simply ignore it. Whoever tries to suppress the nature of the horse will find him- or herself in a dangerous situation at some point.

Info ‖ Common Sense

All equipment used around or on horses has one thing in common: We can do stupid things and cause harm to the horse with any of it if we use it improperly. This rule of course applies to bitless bridles, too. Therefore, before we use a piece of tack or equipment, we have to ask ourselves how it works, what effects it potentially has, and what objectives we want to achieve with it.

Knowledge of the horse's natural predisposition as a flight animal is a (vital!) prerequisite every rider needs to meet—whatever the riding style, and whether with a bridle, bit, and saddle, or without. When you are aware of the fact that you will trigger the flight or fight response in your horse if you treat him roughly or carelessly, you generally behave a little more conscientiously in his presence.

Of course, incorrect behavior on our part does not always trigger panicky flight or defensive behavior in our horse. Flight and fight are extremes in horse behavior, between which any-

thing is possible. The horse's reactions are usually much more subtle—so much so that you would not even notice that you had made a mistake in handling him. Sometimes, you would be surprised how high the horse's level of tolerance really is...

Personally, we find it very unsatisfying to work with a horse that, while he might not be particularly fearful or "spooky," is continuously confrontational and challenges us to a sort of "arm wrestling" match. Horses that are very resistant mentally will have a hard time ever delivering good, relaxed, voluntary performances. Resistance in this case does not necessarily

In this picture, the cheekpiece of the bitless bridle rests a little too close to the horse's eye. This should be corrected through proper adjustment of the cheekpieces and noseband.

express itself as pushing, shoving, or invading your personal space; delayed yielding to slight pressure, for example, is also a form of passive resistance or mental shutdown. The result is lack of suppleness or rideability in your horse, and an uncomfortable and/or "unenjoyable" experience with your horse, whether on the ground or on his back.

The Pros of Riding without a Bit

For many riders, the idea of riding their horse without a bit and defying the traditionally held belief that one is necessary for control and collection is difficult to imagine. Even considering the option seems absurd to most. When we ask riders what they think about riding bitless, we generally hear the same arguments. We also tend to hear the same questions about the possibility. With this pattern in mind, we have compiled these arguments and questions in this book and will discuss some

Human beings are creatures of habit: Often, the only reason we use a bridle with a bit is that we simply always have. It often seems to be a huge mental leap for most riders to imagine the possibility of riding their horse without a bit and the advantages it might offer.

of them in detail. Some of the most frequently asked questions about riding bitless are:

> Isn't this dangerous? How am I supposed to stop my horse in potentially out-of-control situations if he is not wearing a bit?
> How can I collect my horse without a bit?
> Can any horse go bitless?
> Can I trail ride without a bit?
> Do bitless bridles allow for the same degree of precision regarding aids as conventional bridles do?
> Can I retrain my "conventionally" ridden horse to go bitless, and if so, how do I do that?
> Without a bit, my horse does not "champ" and "froth"—so how is he supposed to relax and yield in the poll?
> Are bitless bridles really that much more horse-friendly than those with a bit?

Info Horses Don't Lie

There is always a reason why a horse reacts antagonistically or defensively. Your first step must be to look for the cause—which can usually be found in the handler/rider. Frankly, more pressure (tight nosebands, short side reins, harsh bits) or even punishment/aggression is simply evidence of an uneducated attempt to fight symptoms.

Commonly Heard Advice

In every barn there are those who give advice even when no one asked for it. You probably know the kind of person we are talking about—he or she always has advice handy when someone else has a problem, including where to find the cause and how to fix it.

You may hear recommendations such as: "You just have to show him you are the boss!" or "Why don't you simply tighten that flash?" or "He's totally lacking respect. You have to really stand up to him!" or "You just have to longe him for a while before you get on to really tire him out."

Advice like this is rarely useful and hardly ever addresses the actual root of the problem. Unfortunately, these "helpful" individuals are rarely professionals with any sort of expertise. Most of their advice is based on creating more pressure, which means they don't actually understand the basic principles of normal horse behavior. Trying to "cure" a flight animal by increasing the pressure on him when he does not do what you want is absolute nonsense. As a consequence, horse owners often end up deeply insecure and confused about how to handle their horse and how to solve problems when they arise.

If reasonably trained and kept busy in mind and body, even Thoroughbreds can be calmly and easily controlled with the slightest of aids and little tack. "Less is more!"

Andrea's horse learns to stretch forward-downward while in motion.

When the hands of the rider are sensitive enough, they can "show" the horse how to position his head. No auxiliary rein or training aid can replace the hands of an experienced rider.

Training the Rider

For years, we have been successfully working with horses using an approach that consciously removes all means of coercion, including often the bit. Claiming that problems are generally caused by the bit and that removing it can solve them would be false, however. Things are hardly ever that easy and clear-cut. You always need to take a close look at your horse and figure out the signs he is trying to send you. In other words, you have to try to understand the "story" your horse is telling you. Whenever we discuss a horse's problems with his owner, the owner's conclusions and explanations are always only fragments of the truth, if not completely misleading. You see, the human point of view is rarely identical with the horse's. Therefore, when we take a horse in for training, we rarely ask the rider much and instead let the

When introducing a horse to rein aids, we start by walking right beside his head. Then, over the course of training, we change position and fall a little further back ...

... until we mimic how a rider would be holding the reins from the saddle, as Andrea is demonstrating here.

horse himself tell us his own story, at his own pace. Otherwise, the "case history" the rider has compiled would likely cloud our judgment.

The Art of Small Steps

When we work with allegedly "difficult" horses, we start from scratch and work our way from groundwork into the saddle, taking really small steps. This gives us the opportunity to detect the very first sign of trouble and then locate the problem because we haven't covered so much territory as to make it difficult to determine what may have gone wrong. We proceed from "bottom to top" and "search" the entire horse, which sometimes turns into real detective work: Looking for and finding the tiny puzzle pieces that, when put together correctly, give us a clear overall picture.

Our training proceeds systematically. There are concrete things we ask the

We believe in establishing clear boundaries in a friendly but determined way—just like horses do with one another.

all. In fact, I might just do what they want next time, even if they're asking for a little more!"

The most important thing during the process is to strike a balance: Challenge the horse, but do not to ask too much of him. Your requests should reach the horse's tolerance level (per the respective scenario), but never cross the line beyond and push him too far. In this way, it is possible to slowly build up the horse's tolerance for various situations and increase the scope of his training.

You have probably already noticed that our approach is based on two aspects of the horse's natural behavior: comfort and discomfort. We direct our "energy" toward specific points in order to teach the horse to yield—both mentally and physically. By "energy" we mean different forms of pressure, which can include our breath; focus; body position (such as pointing the front of our body head-on toward horse); varying distance; indirect touches (pointing without actually touching); and direct touches with hands, ropes, or crops.

horse to do and depending on his reaction, we can draw further conclusions—for example, is the horse willing to wait for us when asked; and will he keep a certain distance, obediently follow our lead, and yield to the slightest request?

In the initial phases of training, the demands we make are very small. This way, we increase our chances at receiving the desired reactions from the horse, as well as accomplish two other important things: Firstly, we are able to constantly prove to the horse that we are competent and superior, and have the right to claim the "leading" position in the relationship. This reinforces our credibility and trustworthiness in the eyes of the horse.

Secondly, the horse realizes that the demands we make always appear manageable. He learns that it is not at all difficult, let alone impossible, to satisfy us. By immediately praising him for even the smallest effort to comply with our requests, he quickly gains confidence in us and the entire training situation. We also remove any and all pressure when he reacts correctly. The motivating effect of this approach is amazing. The horse seems to realize: "That wasn't difficult or exhausting at

Info | Find the Right Dosage

The amount of pressure used when asking the horse to complete an exercise is supposed to be high enough to tease out the desired response, but never so great as to trigger retreat, resistance, defense, or aggression in the horse—even when the line between "exactly right" and "too much" is very fine.

As Little as Possible and No More than Necessary!

Working in small steps decreases

the danger of overlooking important parts of your horse's education. Once you have created a solid foundation through groundwork, advancing to a level on which no bridle (or saddle!) is necessary will actually be quite easy.

We have taken the liberty to modify a common basic rule: "As little as possible and no more than necessary!" If auxiliary reins and equipment are superfluous to our style of riding, we are more than happy not to use them. When we look at other riders, however, we realize that most of them do not know how little it takes for their horse to perform what they ask of him correctly. Riders usually do much more than they actually need to!

In this context, the basic principle of applying aids only when necessary holds true—both during groundwork and in the saddle. If the horse does everything we ask him to do, we have to reward his behavior by remaining consciously observant and passive. We do not want to disturb him ("nag" him) unnecessarily. This guiding prin-

ciple enables us to tell the horse much more clearly what he is supposed to do and when.

Performing a movement only when necessary significantly improves body control and the ability to apply precise aids. You need to be able to "feel" how much (or better said, how little) energy you have to expend and when. Knowing the exact moment to yield is equally important. Your body needs to learn how to quickly become active or passive in a controlled manner.

> ### Tip | Yielding from the Handler/Rider's Perspective
>
> The moment the handler/rider yields is fundamental to correct and fair application of the aids. In order to tell my horse that he has just given me a correct response, the fact that I immediately reduce all energy or yield is almost more important than the "active" aid preceding it. Yielding "activates" an active aid.

In this picture, Andrea yields the reins in an exaggerated manner— a useful exercise, especially for beginners who still have to learn how to yield in a timely and sufficient way.

Andrea demonstrates an exercise to develop a feel for the horse's movements: With one hand, clap on your thigh in rhythm with the horse's motion.

Timing and dosage of aids are key to harmonious riding.

Over the years we've employed our method of training, we have come to the conclusion that horses greatly benefit from applying aids in their weakest (meaning most subtle) form. Constantly "harassing" a horse with incessant yet ineffective leg use, in contrast, does him no good. Right from the start, we gently yet firmly encourage the horse to take responsibility for himself. And, getting the intensity of the aids right also means that we learn to support our horse with the minimum of aids needed at exactly the right moment— no less!

Train Your Motor Skills

As riders, we should really be more particular about how we hold and use the reins, since only with trained hands can we enjoy the advantages of a bridle. You do not need a horse to practice the fine motor skills necessary for asking and yielding rein aids. Just find your-

self a partner and a couple of lead ropes, and switch between who plays the role of the horse and who the rider. Provide each other with feedback on how gently or strongly the aids are perceived through the "reins." Targeted exercises to improve coordination help our body in general: What we want is a flexible seat with steady hands.

A good exercise for improving motor skills: While standing, roll loose yarn into a ball. Your body should be positioned upright, your arms relaxed, and your eyes focused on a spot at eye level.

Use a pair of lead rope "reins" to establish very light contact with a human partner. Your task is to react as soon as you feel your partner yield: In turn, your hands have to immediately soften and yield.

Exercises for achieving a better seat: (Left) Andrea is sitting on a specially designed stool called a BALIMO® (Balance in Motion) Chair, which features an unstable seat that is movable in all directions (www.balimochairs.com). At first, simply trying to sit in a normal position poses a challenge—your body has to figure out and develop a feeling for what "sitting straight" actually means.

(Right) Walking on a straight line drawn with chalk helps your body learn how to move at a steady rhythm and in a controlled manner, as well as independent of your line of vision. When you have practiced this simple exercise, it will be easier for your body to flexibly follow your horse's movements and for your hands to remain steady when you are sitting in the saddle.

Improve Your Seat

A prerequisite for steady, gentle hands is developing posture, a seat, that is independent of the reins. The exercises illustrated on these pages will help you in this pursuit.

When we teach students lessons, we like to present the coordination of aids in a specific sequence, particularly with regard to stopping or slowing a horse. These aids are supposed to consist primarily of focus, breathing, voice, weight shifts, and your lower legs. The reins should only be used after all the other aids have been applied. The goal of all of this is precise riding, using no more than necessary.

The bit is not an imperative when it comes to subtle, trusting communica-tion between horse and rider. This is to say that we do not depend on the bit to achieve subtle contact—that is, a dia-log—with the horse. None of the fol-lowing riding goals—understanding, communication, steering, control, edu-cation, training, refinement of the aids—is possible only when using a bit. Each is just as likely to be achieved—and achieved just as well—with a bit-less bridle.

Talking about Contact

When doing research while writing this book and reading professional ar-ticles and books on the topic, we no-ticed that "experts" could not decide

Tie reins or lead ropes to a small plastic garden chair. Gradually shorten your reins, beginning with no contact and proceeding to light contact. Notice how little pull it takes to make the chair slide toward you or topple over. Walk or jog in place and bend your knees into a crouch. You should be able to do so without moving the chair and without losing rein contact.

To increase the level of difficulty, pull on the reins to make the chair tip and rest on the back two legs only. Now repeat the same movements as described above, this time maintaining the chair's unstable balance.

what the point of contact actually is. Is it simply advised, or is it mandatory that you establish rein contact when riding? How does this contact look in practice?

The respected German National Equestrian Federation's (FN) *The Principles of Riding* defines contact as "the soft, steady connection between the rider's hand and the horse's mouth. The horse should go rhythmically forward from the rider's driving aids and 'seek' a contact with the rider's hand, thus

'going onto' the contact." (*The Principles of Riding*. Kenilworth Press, 2003).

When using a bitless bridle, contact in the traditional sense is impossible since it requires the horse to stretch toward the bit (which is missing in this case) and "seek" a certain amount of pressure. Nevertheless, we want to achieve minimal contact with the bridge of the horse's nose, which we encourage by using forward-driving aids. Usually, horses easily and willingly obey.

Light rein contact, a focused expression on the horse's face, and impulsion—aspects of basic horse training that are just as important when you are using a bitless bridle as they are in traditional tack.

In reality, only a few riders are actually able to establish harmonious contact (where the horse can really trust in steady hands) as stipulated by the FN. Let us not sugarcoat things here. The part of the horse most strongly affected by your body is his head (or mouth, when you are using a bit) by way of the reins. This is where the gravest riding mistakes happen, or at least where they have the most significant and visible effects. Therefore, the idea to protect the horse's mouth from the

clumsy or inexperienced hands of riding students is nothing new and it is certainly justified.

We teach a large number of beginners. Naturally, these inexperienced riders make many mistakes—not because they are clumsy or do not try hard enough but because they do not yet know what is important. The mistakes we most commonly observe include difficulty measuring the intensity of the aids and knowing when exactly to apply them. Beginners have not yet developed an understanding for how applying aids should feel when done correctly. Even though all riders have to develop the same set of basic skills to help them navigate around

In the mood for a stretching session? Flexibility and balance are prerequisites for a supple seat and should be practiced on horseback.

The PRE stallion Ginebra used to react defensively to even the slightest pressure from the reins. Baby step by baby step, he learned to relax his neck, stretch forward, and accept and trust the contact offered by his rider's hands. One of the positive effects of this new acceptance of light contact is that he can swing his hind legs further underneath his center of gravity.

horses and in the saddle, each student learns differently. Beginners should have the freedom to express their individuality through systematically structured and varied lessons where they get the chance to learn to find their balance on their horse, develop body awareness, and improve their coordination skills.

Inexperienced riders need to learn to sit without holding on to the reins for balance and they need to practice directing their horses with the subtlest of aids—that is, make use of weight, legs, and focus. They must understand the importance of yielding in the saddle as well as when handling their horse. They should develop a feel for degrees of pressure and perfect their timing, preferably during groundwork and before they get on their horse's back.

Our students learn to always systematically start with the lowest intensity of a request, and then increase it only if necessary. We teach them to recognize every attempt by the horse to do what is asked of him and to immediately reward his behavior by yielding. By

Exercises like circles, serpentines, and changes of pace—even without a bridle—help both horse and rider become better able to perform. In addition, fun and variety are just part of good horse training.

training with exercises on the ground first (see p. 25), beginners should develop a feeling for what subtle contact is supposed to feel like. The same effect can then be reproduced in the saddle later on, at first on a horse that is standing still (static), then in motion.

Once you have mastered all these things, you are no longer a beginner but a highly sensitive and self-controlled rider who has the best chance at getting the horse to do as desired based on his trust and willingness to please you. Irrespective of your riding style, you have established the foundation on which all further training can be based.

The most important lesson for riders to learn is to be flexible. Horses are living beings, after all, and they keep changing constantly. If we force inflexible rules upon them, we restrict and obstruct their learning process.

Info | Collection

Practical experience and the physiological and anatomical structure of the horse's body have shown that contact (in this case, the traditional form of contact with the bit) and collection, as defined by classical dressage, are not integral to keeping a riding horse healthy, happy, and able to carry his rider over many years.

The Horse's Nose...

When we talk about riding with light contact, although without a bit, people sometimes object that the horse would not want to "seek" constant pressure on his nose (as he is thought to "seek" contact with the bit). We are not convinced by this argument. When the bitless bridle is a correct fit, pressure from the

Moraleja, a 24-year-old mare, is one of many horses that we have seen with Serreta scars on their nose (see p. 16). Retraining taught her that being touched on that area of her nose does not necessarily have to be painful. Today, she accepts light contact there, via a bitless bridle, without a problem.

reins does not solely rest on the bridge of the horse's nose but is instead distributed along various areas of the head, including the poll, chin, throat.

Moreover, to us, it seems just as unlikely that the horse "seeks" constant pressure on his tongue, bars, and lower jaw from a metal object inserted into his mouth. It goes without saying that in both cases—with a bit or without—the degree of pressure the horse feels should be as low as possible. Desirable contact is designed to maintain a line of communication between rider and horse; it should never include uncomfortable or even painful pressure.

... His Poor Nose

Riders who prefer bits are often quick to make the following argument: "A bitless bridle could possibly break the horse's nasal bone!" Yes, it's true, devices such as the mechanical hackamore with long levers can indeed break a horse's nasal bone.

A bridle as potentially powerful and sharp as a mechanical hackamore should only be used by a rider with very experienced and sensitive hands and the ability to control them. (Although note that as we mentioned on p. 14, an experienced rider really shouldn't need to use a mechanical hackamore.) The horse that the hackamore is being used on must consistently obey the subtlest of aids. The most important thing about this kind of bridle is who uses it.

Whether it makes sense to use potentially painful devices like a mechanical hackamore at all is another question.

When we compare the areas on the horse's head that receive pressure from the reins in a traditional and a bitless bridle, a significant difference becomes apparent: The bit of a traditional bridle (usually metal), inserted into the horse's mouth, rests on the horse's tongue (large fleshy muscle) and bars (the toothless gap between the incisors and molars of the lower jaw) and often touches the palate. The noseband (reinforced or padded leather) of a bitless bridle rests on the bony part of the bridge of the horse's nose.

The bars of the mouth are narrow bone ridges covered in mucous membrane. Depending on handling and type of bit, the bit itself will have a reasonably strong effect on this area. For physiological reasons, mucous membranes are constantly replaced and regenerated, therefore they cannot develop protective calluses against external forces. It is impossible to enhance their resilience and make them less sensitive—they are forever highly susceptible to pain.

Compared to the bridge of the nose, a (considerably wider) bone covered by skin and hair, the parts of the mouth touched by the bit seem significantly more sensitive and in danger of being negatively affected by the metal that is part of a traditional bridle. (Note that even though the horse's nose is protected by skin and hair, we believe that metal has no business there, either.)

All arguments considered, pain and physical damage appears to be caused more quickly by a bit in the horse's mouth than by a (moderate) bitless bridle that rests on the horse's nose.

Left: The horse's reaction to the rein aids via the bit.

Right: A relaxed, unrestricted mouth.

Where Is the Emergency Brake?

Many people ask us if it is dangerous to ride without a bit—especially out on the trails or in an open field! This question is most commonly asked by people who are fairly experienced riders, and most of them admit having had some bad experience involving a bolting horse in their past. When we ask how they were able to stop their runaway horse, the usual answer is: "Well, I couldn't. My horse didn't respond at all! Whatever I tried, it didn't work."

The story almost always ends in an involuntary return to the barn, or a fall off the horse, or in the best-case scenario, the gradual slowing of the horse after a few hundred yards once his rider was able to regain some degree of control. And in almost every case, the horse was wearing a bit.

As the evidence suggests, even with a metal bit in his mouth, when a horse is out of control the more you pull on the reins, the more the horse accelerates. We can personally attest to this experience—in the past we have found ourselves on the back of a panic-stricken horse racing through a forests at what felt like 60 miles per hour. We know the feeling of helplessness when every attempt at controlling the situation has failed. I also learned about emergency dismount technique the hard way when, on gravel, I boldly jumped off a bolting horse, and my arms and legs left behind some 20 square feet of skin along the ground ...

The point is, once a horse reaches uncontrollable speeds, even a sharp bit does not have any effect. The way you pull on the reins does not make much of a difference either (although admittedly panicky jerks and attempts at staying in the saddle by desperately clinging to the reins are the least productive).

As we've already discussed, horses always react to pain and, or if necessary, frantic flight. When flight is difficult or impossible, horses will fight what scares them. This is one of the reasons why horses cannot really be subdued by inducing pain. At some point, they will simply throw themselves into the source of pain. Their physical superiority in comparison to ours then becomes a serious disadvantage: Muscle strength alone cannot stop the horse.

Now you should easily understand why pulling on or holding on to the reins and the additional pain this creates only increases (or possibly even triggers!) the horse's state of panic. The pain threshold of a horse wearing a bit is definitely crossed more quickly if the reins are handled in an uncontrolled manner. Therefore, a bit must never be your emergency brake as it might fail you and, in fact, increase your chances of further panicking your horse. It would appear that trail rides on well-trained horses wearing bitless bridles are definitely safer!

The Emergency Plan

What are your options in case your horse does decide to move faster than you want him to? Is there an "emergency plan" you can follow?

As we've mentioned, odds are stacked against you once your horse has reached top speed and is unresponsive to any of your signals. At that point, there is little to nothing you can do to make him stop—using mechanical aids, that is. If you fail to make your horse understand that there are good reasons to slow down, you can pull on

Riding is the greatest pleasure we know. The best way to enjoy moments like the one shown here is to train and school your horse well and create a solid relationship between you and your horse.

How does our body react when we get scared? Usually, we instinctively try to protect our vital organs by curling into a ball—not helpful when riding! Here, Andrea demonstrates the countermovement to what we would instinctively do.

the reins as much as you want—to no avail! Bleak prognosis, is it not?

In our humble opinion, most of the well-meant advice, including riding in circles and the like, must be regarded as mere suggestions: Do you believe that in the case of an emergency you will be clear-headed enough to systematically go through your list of braking techniques? Unfortunately, it is unrealistic to try to simulate bolting in order to practice and/or hone your reactions.

Reflex Training

Even though we cannot actually train correct reactions to bolting, we teach our students how to influence their own reflexes in emergency situations. When you become insecure, scared, or startled, your body's automatic reaction to protect its vital organs is to curl into a ball.

This means that you bend forward, curl, and pull your arms and legs toward your body in a reflex motion. Otherwise a useful mechanism of protection, this behavior generally has negative effects on riding: You lose your balance and are easily propelled forward over your horse's neck. In addition, jerking your arms backward toward your body most certainly causes great discomfort or even pain to your horse's mouth. And, latching onto your horse's body with your legs does not make it more likely for you to stay in the saddle but most certainly accelerates your horse's speed!

All of the protective positions inspired by panic that I've just described have fatal effects on a horse that is already bolting. So the first and most important suggestion for what to do when your horse bolts is: Keep calm! This is easy to say yet difficult to put into practice during an actual emergency, we know. We find it is useful to concentrate on one specific thought—that is, by focusing your thoughts on something specific, it is possible to prevent yourself from slipping into a state of blind panic. Personally, we remind ourselves that where we live, our horses have no actual life-threatening reasons to take off in mindless flight. This thought helps us concentrate on conveying our certainty to our horse, and feeling that we are responsible for the safety of our horse turns into a concrete task we can concentrate on. In this way, we do "not have the time" to panic.

Even though not everyone is equally good at staying calm, our form of "reflex training" can help keep you safe. After we explain our physical reaction to threat (protect our vital organs—see p. 36), we practice countermovements. These include leaning backward instead of forward, stretching the arms forward, and pushing the feet forward-and-downward into the stirrups.

Leaning backward helps you better maintain a deep and stable position in the saddle. Stretching your arms loosens the reins and/or prevents jerking on them. Keeping your legs "away" from your horse's body prevents you from (involuntarily) telling him to go even faster.

During lessons, we teach our students to perform these countermovements when they hear a previously determined acoustic signal such as, for example, hands clapping, or a certain word called out. The most important part of this exercise is to have an immediate reaction to the audible cue. Giving up the reins can also be taught in a playful manner. This enables us to immediately assume a safe position in the saddle if need be and to prevent dangerous reactions such as pulling on the reins or holding on to them in panic. A stable position in the saddle can be all we need to maintain a sense of calm in a bolting situation.

Interval Braking

Another technique to add to your reflex training repertoire is a kind of "ABS" (anti-lock) braking system used in combination with exerting pressure on only one rein. After you have learned to give up the reins completely, you need to be able to quickly but gently pick them up again, then brake in intervals, pulling back and then yielding. This technique prevents you from creating resistance in your horse, as you do when you constantly pull on or hang on the reins. By repeatedly applying the braking aids, the probability of reestablishing your horse's suppleness (in body and mind) is much higher.

One-sided rein aids have a similar effect to your ABS system. The prerequisite, however, is perfectly trained

Left: Braking is not just about "pulling on the reins." Proper interval braking consists of tightening and loosening the reins, in combination with other aids.

Right: Once the horse has stopped, yielding with your hands marks the completion of halt.

lateral flexion or bend. Practice this in a stress-free arena—the better and quicker you can make your horse bend and take a sharp turn by exerting pressure on just one rein, the greater the probability that this maneuver will disrupt his forward drive in a runaway situation. You rather elegantly "stall" his engine.

The better the aforementioned exercises work under "normal" circumstances, the more likely they will help you in the case of an actual emergency. It is an advantage if your horse is familiar with the aids and maneuvers, as he is then more likely to allow you to reestablish control.

Basic Exercise: Halt and Wait

What is more important than knowing how to handle an emergency? Actually preventing it in the first place by training your horse well—first on the ground, and later in the saddle. Because uncontrolled situations can prove life-threatening to us, we make a point of providing our horses with a thorough

and functional groundwork schooling or "education." This is actually the only "brake" that is truly effective.

Practice this basic exercise: Make it a habit to ask your horse to come to a complete stop in any situation imaginable. Then let him stand still and wait for a few seconds. What he is supposed to learn is that you always have the right to make him stop, no matter the circumstances. It is not enough to practice in the arena where your horse willingly complies when in other situations he fidgets and impatiently pulls on the lead rope. He should halt and wait on command on the way to the barn, the pasture, or long-awaited food. Does your horse stop on command when the two of you go for a walk and you ask him to halt for a few seconds? Does he patiently wait for you to allow him to lower his head to graze? Will your horse wait until you give him a bucket filled with food or treats, or is he pushy? Has he learned to stand still while you mount or does he walk away before you are seated? When you stop

injuries and several hospitalizations.

We will never be able to erase the innate and natural flight instinct in a flight animal. What we can do, however, is to turn the horse into a reasonably safe mount by providing him with sound habits of obedience and training under saddle that takes his natural behavior into consideration.

Bitless—A Carte Blanche?

As we discussed earlier, bitless bridles are not necessarily more horse-friendly than those with bits. You do not want a bridle's effects to simply move from the mouth to the bridge of the nose. A good bridle distributes its pressure over different areas of the horse's head without creating any pressure "peaks." In order for your bridle to fulfill this purpose, you need to read up on all the different kinds available and how they work. You also need to learn how to correctly fit a bridle. HOW you use the bridle—whatever kind it is—is up to you.

We pity those horses that wear bitless bridles and are still, despite the lack of bit, being tortured with them. In such cases, the rider has failed to understand the effect of the bridle. We also feel sorry for horses that, despite going bitless, move on the forehand, shuffle around with inactive hindquarters, bend with the flexibility of a highway guard rail, are completely stiff in their head and neck, and have never experienced the feeling of stretching their topline.

In both cases, the cause or responsibility, respectively, for the grievance lies with the rider. Riding without a bit does not mean we have been handed a carte blanche that frees us from the responsibility of educating ourselves and gymnasticizing our horses.

Info | Gymnasticizing

It is possible to gently train and effectively "gymnasticize" horses, even when they are not wearing a bit. Gymnasticizing is defined as exercising a horse in a way that allows him to redistribute his balance under his rider. By building up his muscles correctly, you enable your horse's body to carry you without sustaining injuries. The best way to achieve this is to practice exercises in which your horse learns to bend, such as circles, serpentines, and lateral work. Asking him to actively go forward while stretching his topline forward-downward is another very effective gymnasticizing exercise.

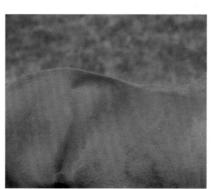

Left: The back of this horse was sore and dropped after years of premature training, incorrect usage, and a rough style of riding.

Right: Through correct training, the back is now ready to withstand the normal "wear-and-tear" caused by riding.

"Bitless" Doesn't Mean "Contactless"

Just because you choose not to use a bit does not mean that you should simply keep the reins long and stroll through the woods. The conclusion that we do not want any contact at all because we are not looking for contact in the traditional sense (via a bit) is false. Using a bitless bridle, we still wish to maintain a subtle, if intermittent contact. There should be a minimal connection between our hands and the horse's head by way of reins. This slight contact should never disturb, interfere with, or slow down your horse ("slow down" in the sense of pulling the reins toward you). However, your sensitive hands are still expected to control the vertical and lateral position of your horse's head and neck at all times.

By "releasing" or yielding the reins regularly, you can check to make sure your horse is "carrying" himself or if he is stiff and depends on the reins for support.

We also use the reins to influence the flexibility and correct the position of the horse's forehand. In order to do this, we need a minimum of contact, which must never become inflexible, especially when the horse tenses up.

Flex and Relax

In order to prevent tension from developing in the horse, we include transitions from muscle flexion to relaxation and back again more frequently than most trainers—approximately every one or two minutes, sometimes even more often. We might, for example, ask the horse to stretch his topline while maintaining the same degree of impulsion from his hindquarters. Frequent "releases" or yielding of the reins also helps get rid of stiffness and excessive tension.

The more you and your horse practice changing between flexing and relaxing, the easier it will become for your horse to work on the dynamic stability of his topline and to slightly increase the basic level of "positive" tension in this area. The aids that you apply when asking your horse to flex and relax have a gymnasticizing effect, and moreover, your horse does not get the chance to lean on the reins. Instead, he quickly and independently establishes his own balance. The flexibility of his head and neck, which we improved on the ground early in training (see p. 8), contributes to his balance to a significant degree.

Your hands play an important part in the flex-and-relax exercise. They need to be sensitive, dynamic, and stable so that they can reward your horse every time he yields by yielding in return—gently and lightly. (You might have to open your fingers slightly.) This

applies in situations where your horse, for example, yields in the poll.

As a rider, you also have to learn to sense how long your horse is able to maintain the frame you desire (that is, "self-carriage") and when he is starting to get tired. You want to request active relaxation before he is exhausted.

The goal of riding bitless, and with a bit, is to focus on your line of vision, weight, and legs, so that rein aids only play a supporting role in your riding. As you might have realized, riding correctly, precisely, with the subtlest of aids and in dialog with your horse, is just as demanding without a bit as it is with.

In an article written about different kinds of bridles, German trainer Angelika Weinzierl commented: "Unfortunately, most people forget that you need to have an exceptionally stable seat, without using the reins for balance, if you want to train or retrain a horse without a bit. You must never under any circumstances hold on to the reins for balance." We find this an interesting statement, as should it not be the goal of every riding style that riders develop an (almost) rein-independent seat

Andrea demonstrates stiff, unyielding hands—what the hands of good riders should NOT look like!

so their hands work gently and the contact is soft? And have you ever actually heard of a riding style that allows its riders to use the reins for balance? We have not.

In our opinion, bitless riding offers the additional benefit of teaching riders to establish a stable and balanced seat much more quickly. Because they don't have to worry about their seat, they have time to concentrate on how to hold and use the reins. Unfortunately, this still hasn't become our riding culture "norm." Instead, we usually see unbalanced riders with the reins in a death grip, no sign of gentle contact, and a desperate horse busy going through his entire repertoire of mouth twists and tongue movements to avoid discomfort. In these cases, the damage easily done by a bit in the wrong hands is obvious.

Info Muscles

Muscles work rhythmically, constantly changing between states of flexion and relaxation (or stretching, respectively). Whenever a muscle is stretched or flexed for too long, the demands become physiologically unsustainable. Oxygen supply and/or removal of carbon dioxide is obstructed (the muscles receive too little oxygen and too much carbon dioxide, which negatively affects their performance). As a consequence, the body needs more energy to do the same amount of work.

The subtle, harmonious interplay of all aids—weight, legs, and reins—at the right moment is a constantly changing "conversation." Here, Andrea is too "constant" with all her aids at the same time.

Precise Aids

The riding aids consist of weight aids, leg aids, and rein aids. Weight and leg aids are supposed to dominate; we strive for a harmonious interplay of all of them.

The hands are in charge of maintaining a direct line of communication to the horse's head. We want to establish and sustain a subtle and gentle connection or "friendly contact."

As mentioned before, it is this gentle and precise use of the reins that is impossible for most riders to put into practice. The impulses sent from reins to bit, which in traditional bridles affect the very sensitive mouth of the horse, often are of an inadequate and uncontrolled nature, and usually, they are too strong. We doubt that they translate the rider's wishes as precisely and finely nuanced as intended. Only the disciplined hands of professional riders are usually able to do so.

Riders using bits often argue (illogically) that horses trained with bitless bridles, in particular, have to be controlled with "exceptional precision" as they would otherwise be "too danger-ous." As you know by now, there is no reason to think that precision standards with a bit are any different without one—either way subtlety and comfort of the horse are paramount.

"Champing" the Bit and Relaxing in the Poll

Should horses "champ" or chew the bit and foam slightly at the mouth when being ridden, or not? This is another one of those commonly argued topics among riders.

We feel that moderate amounts of champing and a little bit of foam during intense riding sessions are acceptable. Ideally, the horse looks like he is wearing a touch of white lipstick. Moderate chewing is a sign of relaxation and flexibility in the jaws. The jaws are the key to the horse's poll: If the jaws remain loose and flexible, the neck muscles relax as well, and the excretory ducts of the parotid glands (located underneath the jaws) open up and cause an increase in salivation. As a matter of fact, increased chewing and a moderate build-up of foam around the mouth might as well be considered an

In contrast to the photograph on p. 44, here you can see how Andrea is giving her horse a little more space by extending her arms and taking pressure off the reins. As a result, the horse's forward movement and forward thrust immediately improve.

indication that the horse is yielding at the poll. This explains why moderate chewing and a frothy line along the lips can be seen in horses wearing a bitless bridle.

Excessive foaming and nervous champing at the bit, however, is undesirable and rather pointless. It is a sign of a horse not being relaxed. If you take a look at the rest of the horse's body, you will probably find more indicators pointing to tension: tense muscles in the face and underside of neck; a stiff and hollow back; tentative movements; hind legs that do stride under the horse's center of gravity; and so on. Using your hands and reins to encourage excessive chewing on the bit does not necessarily prove that you are doing a good job since all you might be showing is your horse's attempt to get rid of the bit and its feeling in his mouth.

As a result of subtle rein aids and active forward-driving aids, you may see some champing and a little bit of white foam along the horse's lips, even when a bitless bridle is used.

Left: Fabiola's reacts to being stroked on the neck with visible stretching.

Right: Even though the reins are loose, Fabiola's topline remains slightly stretched. When the horse is moving, we do not yield as much as shown in this picture at the halt.

We want to achieve and maintain complete flexibility in the horse's head and neck (for reasons of balance, among others). Frequently changing between "asking" and "yielding" rein aids ("playing around with the reins") while the horse continues to move forward actively, quickly induces chewing, signaling this flexibility. We also may repeatedly stroke or "massage" both sides of the horse's neck, moving parallel to the crest in order to get the horse to chew, yield in the poll, and relax the muscles in his neck without losing positive tension along his topline. Tense horses, in particular, react most noticeably to this method, which seems to help them relax more quickly.

Relaxation and yielding in the poll are often difficult or almost impossible to regain once horses have had a negative or painful experience with a bit or a rider with insensitive hands. The horse seems to lose faith in his ability to relax. Horses wearing bitless bridles are generally more relaxed in neck, poll, and head, which is why they often tend to yield more quickly. Of course, the skills and behavior of the rider play an important role in this matter.

The Bit—Still a Restraint in Your Mind

Riders constantly confirm our theory that they only use a bit because they "feel a little safer with it." They often even admit that they are aware that this is all in their head and has nothing to do with their horse! We now also know it is false to claim that a bitless bridle does not allow for aid application as precise as a traditional bit does. Aids should always be easy for the horse to understand because we expect him to quickly accept them and obey them so we can ride precise arena figures and exercises. At the same time, the interplay of the aids is supposed to be almost invisible. Applying precise aids is a fundamental safety aspect all riding styles should make one of their priorities. Based on all of this, the kind of bridle the horse uses should really not matter at all.

We repeat: Systematic, individually adapted training and education of horse and rider should replace the constant discussions over whether to use a bit or not. It is not the tool that is important, but the manner in which it is

used—and it is this that needs to be practiced and taught much more intensely. The head and mind is where the horse should first and foremost accept the aids (that is, he should willingly abide by the rider's wishes); as a result, the rest of his body will follow suit. The only way we can truly control the horse is to access his mind. He needs to find great comfort in what we ask of him so that he "gives" us control over his body.

A Game of Q & A

After teaching your horse to automatically lower his head when subtle rein aids ask him to do so (see p. 11), you can move on to practicing the same move under saddle. This exercise is the first step toward teaching your horse to stretch forward-downward with you on board.

Start by practicing while your horse is standing still. This is the easiest way for you and your horse to communicate and for you to observe the "conversation" without the additional destabilizing effect of motion. We like to subdivide the often very complex motion sequences of riding into smaller, manageable steps. We start by working on the ground, then move on to sitting on a horse at halt, then to walk, trot, and, finally, canter.

First, establish very light contact by picking up both reins and holding them one in each hand. The reins should be long enough so you do not have any contact with your horse's head. Make sure that your hands are positioned correctly with relaxed, upright fists held just in front of your belly button. One way to check if you are doing this correctly is to shake the reins a little: They should be loose enough so the only weight you feel is the weight of the reins themselves.

Next, slowly move your hands closer to your belly button. The second you sense slight resistance, stop. This is when you have reached a position of minimal contact with the horse's head. We are not talking about pulling the horse's head backward but about finding a subtle connection. Repeat the movement several times with your eyes closed to develop a feeling for the difference between the weight of the reins only (no contact) as opposed to a slight resistance (subtle contact).

Left: We want to develop a feeling for the weight of the reins without contact with the horse's mouth ...

Right: ... in order to be able to recognize the difference when the hands have been moved slightly backward to create a subtle connection. Note how the slightest difference in hand position causes a change in posture in the sensitive horse shown here.

Top: "Playing with" the reins influences the position of the horse's head. Here, Fabiola yields in the poll.

Bottom: In order for Fabiola to learn to lower her head and neck in an even more relaxed manner, Andrea bends the mare's neck sideways while massaging the crest.

aids are too strong, perhaps pulling the horse's head backward. Your goal is for your horse to slightly yield in the poll—it will look like he is nodding a little. The muscles on the underside of his neck relax while those on the upper side develop "positive" tension: From the saddle, it will look like your horse's mane is arching toward you.

The most important thing to look for, however, is that your horse's head nods downward-forward. If he does not yet understand this exercise he might not yield immediately, or he may offer you some alternative reactions. Be patient and keep asking your horse to yield with your reins. Note: The easier it was to teach him this exercise during groundwork, the quicker he will understand under saddle.

Be prepared for the fact that your horse is most likely going to look for the right answer and suddenly present it to you. You need to be prepared for this moment: Immediately and exaggeratedly move your hands forward and down in order to reward his behavior. Praise him effusively. Repeat the same exercise several times:

   1 Establish minimal contact.

   2 "Play with" (tug on) the reins to ask for yielding.

   3 Reward the correct reaction with immediate pressure reduction.

Ideally, you will notice that your horse reacts more quickly and easily with each repetition. If you notice him chewing or licking after a repetition, wait until he is finished; he is busy digesting what he has just learned. Do not interrupt his learning process.

When he is done, ask him to walk forward a few steps, halt, and repeat the exercise so he again yields to the reins. During early training, it does not mat-

Once you have established the desired contact, alternately tug a little on each rein the way you did during groundwork (see p. 11). Make sure that you maintain minimal contact: If you lose the connection, your horse has no reason to react to your commands. The tugging motions should originate in your fingers or hands, not in your arms as often seen in riders who are "seesawing."

If the contact causes your horse to move backward, close your legs lightly around his body. Check if your rein

ter if your horse does not stay in the same position once you reduce rein pressure. Yield your hands in an exaggerated manner even if this means that your horse's head moves up or he stretches his head and neck forward-downward. What you really want to teach your horse is to yield when you tug on the reins. If he does this correctly, even just for a second, your primary goal has been achieved. Make sure you immediately reward his behavior by yielding the reins!

Yielding at the Walk

Once your horse understands what you want, and your hands have become sensitive enough to immediately yield the reins in reply to your horse's yield, you can practice the Game of Q & A at the walk.

Make sure your horse's walk is brisk: This is the only way to produce enough forward thrust and activity in the hindquarters to push the horse's body toward the bit or bridle. After all, the hindquarters constitute a large part of the arc of "positive" tension that runs from head to tail (the topline). Your goal is to encourage your horse to stretch forward-downward while in motion. The more quickly he learns to yield and stretch forward toward his end of the reins, the sooner you can extend the duration you ask him to stay in this position.

Pay attention to the form of your horse's neck when he stretches. You should see an even arch running from poll to withers. The poll must always remain the highest point in the horse, even when he yields there; otherwise, you will see a "broken neckline" where your horse yields too much in the area of the first few cervical vertebrae, causing his forehead to move behind the vertical (slightly in front is perfect) and preventing him from building "positive" tension in his topline.

Once your horse has learned the correct position, ask him to maintain it for a few seconds. In order to do this, keep your hands soft but steady. Only after he remains in the requested position for a few seconds should you yield the reins. Proceed according to our principle emphasizing the "art of small steps": Practice at a halt, then move on to walk, always asking for your horse to maintain the position just a little bit longer. At this point in training, do not give in to the temptation of asking your horse to go round the arena maintaining "positive" tension in his topline without a break. The only outcome will be resistance and "negative" tension in your horse.

Your need to develop a feeling for the exact moment when your horse is no longer able to maintain the desired position in a relaxed and supple manner. Precisely at that point, you need to yield. This way, your horse learns that he can actively carry himself in a forward-downward frame and that resistance (on his part) is unnecessary. His body receives a physiologically positive and beneficial workout.

The reflex training we described earlier (see p. 25) plays a fundamental role in this process. It is helpful to practice the exercise on the ground with a partner before you get on your horse. Use lead ropes or reins and learn to sense the slightest degree of yielding on your partner's part. Close your eyes, and practice first while standing still before repeating the exercise while walking around. When you start moving, it is much more difficult to feel small changes in pressure—this is when you need to use all your senses.

Further Exercises

> Ask your horse to yield in the poll while walking briskly.
> At a halt, ask your horse to yield in the poll, then ask him to hold that position as he takes a few energetic steps forward at the walk. This significantly increases the level of difficulty involving balance and "positive" tension, and your horse will learn to use his hindquarters to develop more impulsion.
> First at a halt, later at the walk: Combine yielding in the poll with lateral flexion—that is, teach your horse to stretch forward-downward and yield sideways at the same time. In the beginning, only ask for slight lateral flexion so you do not disturb your horse's balance.
> Increase the level of difficulty of all the forward-downward and poll-yielding exercises. Practice at the trot and, later, at the canter. Abide by our principle that the better your horse succeeded at the previous (easier) step, the more quickly you can increase the level of difficulty and proceed to the next one. Be careful, though—it often happens that our lack of self-discipline plays a mean trick on us: Because things are going so well, we may want to do just one more repetition, and then another one, and another, until suddenly we have overdone it.
> At a medium walk or trot, ask your horse to stretch forward-downward as much as possible. Note: You want him to stretch toward the bit or bridle; you do not want him to pull the reins out of your hands!
> Practice the gentle transition between a good stretching position and a more collected one. Switch back and forth between the two.
> Once your horse is able to maintain the desired position (self-carriage) for a few seconds at least, ask him for pace variations within the gaits. Again, pay attention! Please do not miss the moment when your horse gets tired. And the first few times you do this exercise should last no more than a few seconds.
> Transition to a halt. If your horse lifts his head and loses the desired position, remind him to yield. Only walk on again once he has yielded. It should become increasingly more natural for your horse to transition to a halt while yielding at the poll. The difficulty here is you do not want to increase the amount of rein pressure you apply.
> Once your transitions to a halt have become soft and precise, ask your horse to yield in the poll before you give the signal to move forward. Your horse should maintain the same head and neck position. This variation teaches him to use his hindquarters to push his body forward.

The "Flash"—A Way to Camouflage Symptoms

We have often observed the following scenario: A rider with unyielding hands causes resistance in the horse. The horse tries to avoid the pain in his mouth by twisting and turning his mouth and tongue. The rider's answer to this problem is to add a (too) tightly fastened flash strap to the bridle the next time he rides to keep the horse from repeating the undesired behavior. (It should be noted that flash straps used too tightly also stop the horse from the desired chewing and foaming motions—see p. 44.)

Left: Andrea practices flexing and bending under saddle, a logical continuation of our groundwork exercises (see p. 11).

Below: Increased lateral flexion and bend should be achieved gently and should not require any physical effort on our part. These pictures clearly show the horse's willingness to participate in the exercise. Increased lateral flexion requires the horse to develop good balancing skills, so note that this can be a demanding exercise. Be aware that the inability to bend is not necessarily a sign of lack of respect on the part of the horse.

Here you can see the result of our exercises that develop and promote suppleness in the horse: Moraleja canters in a beautiful frame. The loose reins indicate that she is well balanced and "carrying herself."

Your horse will always be stronger than you, whether he is aware of that fact or not. We cannot rely on "tricking" or outwitting him to get him to cooperate. Our goal must be to get him to actively participate, to be alert and "present," and to "think for himself." When he mentally "invests" in your work, you and your behavior will be able to convince him that obeying you pays off. As trainer Pat Parelli says, "We can't force a horse to like us, but we can nudge him in that direction and influence him accordingly."

Info   "Unintentional" Lessons

When you are trying to "actively" or consciously teach your horse new things, it is not necessarily only those lessons that he will eventually remember. Horses just as quickly pick up on things you unknowingly reinforce by neglecting to correct them (often because of inconsistency)—regardless of whether you are aware of it or not.

It is dangerous to believe that you can really control your horse by using a certain type of equipment. Perhaps you think, "This way I can stop him more easily when he spooks or bolts!" Whoever says and seriously believes this is taking an enormous safety risk, however.

As we've mentioned, the goal of our training method is not to find the right combination of tack and equipment to keep our horse under control, but instead to find the root of control problems: Why does he want to or think he has to run away? If we pay attention, our horse gives us the first hints as to why training issues might exist during groundwork. It is there that we must make the horse understand that there

"A Horse Must Never Know How Strong He Is!"

If we tried to physically fight 1,000 (or more) pounds of live weight, we would definitely end up the loser. Our only chance to gain a minimum of control when working with our horse is not to use yet another strap or training device, but instead to convince our horse—on a nonphysical level—that there is no need for him to resist or fight us.

is no need to flee or fight, but just the opposite: There are very good reasons to listen to us.

Exercises

Mounting and Waiting

We must teach our horse to stand still while and right after we get into the saddle. He should wait for our signal instead of just moving ahead by himself. This training issue is quite common and is usually caused by a lack of consistency on the part of the rider, both in the saddle and on the ground.

We hope it has become clear why we set such great store in the basic training and schooling the horse receives during groundwork. The successful completion of many under-saddle exercises depends on whether we consistently practiced them on the ground first. When our horse has learned to halt and wait in hand, whenever we ask and wherever we are (see p. 38), he will most likely also remain patient while we are mounting. This is an example of a good habit developed through groundwork and continued under saddle.

Mounting and Waiting: How It Is Done

When teaching the horse to wait while mounting, the reins should have a light contact with the horse's mouth and/or head. Eventually, however, the goal is to have a horse that stands still with no rein contact at all.

When you have to keep the reins tight while adjusting your equipment, you have (perhaps without knowing it) developed a common bad habit. While you tried to prevent your horse from moving, he learned to interpret loose reins as a signal to start walking. Con-

sequently, he will only "wait" if the "handbrake" is applied.

This is, once again, a question of habit: Riding styles often focus very strongly on the reins, which are mostly used for slowing down and/or stopping the horse. The horse then feels like he is constantly prevented from going forward. As we discussed earlier, it is intrinsic to the horse's nature to resist

It is important that the horse learns to wait after you've mounted. Every attempt at walking forward (without having been asked) must be quickly corrected and the desired reaction rewarded with an immediate yielding of the reins.

persistent forms of energy (such as pressure or pull), and his automatic reaction to constant rein pressure will first be mental (in the form of passive resistance) before it turns physical and encompasses his entire body. This means that the horse will permanently fight the reins, maybe expressed as a heavy weight you feel resting on the reins (leaning on the bit or bridle), maybe as head shaking, or as pulling the reins from your hands.

To us, precise and consistent halting and patient waiting looks very different than the above scenario of holding tight to the reins. We want the horse to "understand" that his rider has asked him to stand still. Do not mistake "preventing a horse from stepping forward" with training a horse to halt correctly. The ability to get our horse to stand still in a calm and relaxed manner with loose reins and no signs of agitation—so we can settle in the saddle, or fix our equipment or clothes, for example—is important not only for safety reasons, but as a step in our horse's understanding of what we expect of him.

Transition to Walk

When you are ready to ask your horse to transition from halt to walk, what do you do first?

No, please do not let the first thing you do be kicking your horse with your heels! Our students soon learn what we expect them to say: "First, I picture exactly what I am going to do. I come up with a plan!"

A clearly defined thought is the first aid you need to apply for every exercise. The clearer the image in your mind, the more quickly your body will be able to transform your intention into "positive" tension, motion, and action. Remember our earlier lesson about being emotionally "collected" (see p. 6).

Transition to Walk: How It Is Done

Focus your thoughts on the first step you want your horse to take, which should be relaxed but brisk. Take a deep breath and direct your eyes in the direction you intend to ride.

Slightly increase your overall body tension and make sure your lower legs are in contact with your horse's sides. Your heels should be low, which creates light tension in your calf muscles and turns the subtle contact between lower leg and horse into little more than mere tension (as opposed to pressure). Use your lower legs a little behind the girth, as the horse's stomach is much more sensitive behind the ribs. In this way, your aid application will succeed with significantly subtler aids. Your upper body and reins remain mostly passive during this exercise, although you can feel free to click your tongue or use a voice command to encourage your horse to walk.

Once your horse has willingly obeyed your request to walk, make sure horse and gait are eager and lively. The walk is the basic gait that paves the way to all the other gaits and exercises. Your horse is much more willing to transition up to faster gaits when he realizes that the two of you are able to effortlessly and consistently establish a brisk walk. At the same time, you are developing your horse's hindquarter impulsion. Your horse will swing his hind legs further underneath his center of gravity at a brisk walk.

Once your horse has learned to move forward at a brisk and eager walk (which, through consistent training, will soon become a habit), you have to behave like an "active spectator." Avoid constantly kicking your horse with your heels in order to keep him going. As soon as your horse has reacted as desired, do what you always do: Decrease pressure, energy, and activity to let your horse know that he has done exactly what you wanted him to do. Remain alert and attentive, and always ready to take action if necessary.

The last two words we want to emphasize: Only take action if you have to. The second your horse thinks about slowing down, you need to apply well-adjusted forward-driving aids. If you do this at the right moment, your aids will be almost invisible because they can be very subtle. "In life, the right moment—perfect timing—always comes sooner than we expect!"

If you apply aids only after your horse has already stopped, you have missed the right moment. "Right" in this context means the point of highest effectiveness. With regard to horse training and handling, timing and "dosage" of the aids (that is, doing the right thing at the right time) are two key ideas you will come across again and again.

Aim to apply your aids efficiently and only when necessary. The rest of the time, keep still and do not pester your horse by moving around your arms and/or legs. This makes it easier for the horse to understand what you expect from him and gives you more time to concentrate on your seat, breathing, and focus, so you are better prepared to move into action when necessary.

As soon as Moraleja responds correctly and starts to walk on cue, Andrea's forward-driving aids turn into "observing-guarding" aids. Constant kicking with your heels or pressure from your lower legs only makes your horse insensitive to the aids.

The prerequisite for a correct halt is an energetic walk: The better the walk, the more precise the subsequent halt.

Halt

It is easier to halt when the horse is alert and actively moving forward at the walk. This might seem like a contradiction since it seems a rider would want to slow down in order to eventually come to a halt. Why is it, then, that the first thing you do to transition to halt is get your horse to actively walk forward?

To us, a good, energetic walk is characterized by a horse that places his hooves in a mindful and focused manner. He is alert and coordinates his movements at every step. A good walk is not simply about speed as measured in miles per hour but about a horse being mentally and physically alert. Only horses that pay attention are able to notice your subtle commands; and only if their body is ready to act will they be able to coordinate their movements in a way that allows for a precise transition to a halt at any given point.

To many, horses often seem insensitive and stolid. We frequently hear comments like "He has a thick skin," or "I have to make myself really clear in order to get a reaction out of him." According to our experience, there are no insensitive horses. Unfortunately, how-ever, there are many horses that have systematically been dulled or "desensitized"—even if not on purpose. This is often a result of riding "mindlessly," particularly when it comes to the forward-driving aids. Applying these aids simply as a matter of principle and irritating your horse by constantly bumping your legs against his sides renders your aids useless as your horse is progressively desensitized to them.

When you mindlessly apply forward-driving aids all the time, it becomes near impossible for you to notice when your horse reacts to your aids the way you want him to, and therefore you never give your horse any straightforward confirmation as to whether his behavior is correct or not. If you keep applying (pointless!) leg aids, you leave it up to your horse to take a guess at the right "answer" (reaction) to your "question" (cue). You expect your horse to immediately and precisely react, but to what exactly? Desired behavior will increasingly depend on flukes, while your horse gets more and more confused, eventually becoming unmotivated and insubordinate.

Permanent pressure eventually causes resistance in your horse. Precisely relieving pressure—in the case of this exercise, immediately ceasing the use of your forward-driving aids when he moves at the desired speed—provides clarity and makes precise riding possible.

Put another way, you want to emphasize and practice the necessity of only acting when the situation requires you to do so and otherwise keeping still and observing. Immediately after having applied all forward-driving aids and received a correct response, your lower leg, which you had pressed lightly against your horse's sides, relaxes and becomes passive.

Do you remember the heading of this section? It was, "Halt." The fact that we have been talking about forward-driving aids so much shows again where the halt actually begins—and it is not with non-yielding rein aids.

When your horse is attentive and walks briskly because he understands that he is supposed to, he will also react to subtle aids meant to make him halt. Another advantage of an attentive horse is that he will react significantly more quickly to subtler aids as he will recognize them sooner than an inattentive horse would. Making it a habit to remain attentive keeps your horse sensitive—a lack of attention on his part always results in a lack of sensitivity. A lazy horse shuffling around the arena is neither paying attention nor sensitive.

It is up to you to keep your horse sensitive. It is usually us and our lack of perception that cause our horses to become stolid.

Remember the importance of timing and dosage—recognizing the perfect moment to act or not to act. Naturally, this basic principle not only applies to the art of applying forward-driving aids and transitioning to halt, but to all other areas of riding as well.

Halt: How It Is Done

During groundwork, your horse learned to always pay attention to you so that, at this point, he should recognize and remember the very first aid he ever encountered. Do you remember it, as well?

In order to halt, the first thing you have to do is create a plan or image in your mind of where you want your horse to stop and stand still. Breathe out and allow yourself to sink deeper into the saddle. Sitting deep in the saddle has a sort of "hind leg brake" effect on your horse. You can increase this effect even more by "growing your heels downward." By slightly stretching your legs down a little further, you automatically sit deeper in the saddle. (Note: Make sure, however, that you do not put more weight or pressure on your stirrups, as this has the opposite effect and raises you out of the saddle.)

As before, feel free to use a vocal cue in addition to your leg and seat aids. Slightly delay the use of your rein aids to see if you really need them. Then, gently but continually increase the pull on the reins until your horse has actually come to a halt.

The very last aid you have to apply in order to halt is yielding—ceasing all aids that are telling the horse to slow down. This acknowledges the successful outcome of the exercise—a full halt. Your horse will quickly realize that when he obeys and halts, he can enjoy the decrease in intensity of aids, especially the rein aids, that reward his correct reaction. He will also desire the related moment of relaxation that follows. Soon, your horse will find it desirable to halt and stand still on a loose rein.

Rein-Back

Once you have taught your horse to halt and remain standing, you can teach him the rein-back. At first, we prefer to clearly separate halt and rein-back so as not to confuse the horse.

This means that you should only apply the rein-back aids after your horse has come to a full stop and you have yielded to reward him.

Rein-Back: How It Is Done

Remember to first mentally prepare yourself for asking your horse to back up. Both reins should be in light contact with your horse's head while your lower legs slide into a guarding position (see photo p. 55). Lean slightly forward to relieve your horse's hindquarters of your weight so they are free to move backward.

Apply pressure with your lower legs. If your horse's reaction is to step forward, your reins should prevent him from doing so. He will realize that the path in front of him is "closed" as are the ones to the either side (as they are "guarded" by your legs).

Be patient if your horse is not yet familiar with the exercise. Apply your aids until he moves in the only possible direction: backward. As usual, your automatic reaction must be to immediately yield and decrease the intensity of your aids. Praise your horse.

It is important that you do not re-

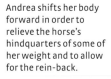

Andrea shifts her body forward in order to relieve the horse's hindquarters of some of her weight and to allow for the rein-back.

flexively pull on the reins if he does not offer the desired response right away. You want your horse to back up with his back rounded and without lifting his head. You have a better chance of achieving this when using your weight and legs, to ask for rein-back, rather than just rein pressure. Even though pulling back on the reins might work, it usually builds up resistance in the horse. He will try to avoid the rein pressure by lifting his head and lowering his back—the opposite of what you want. (Note: This tendency is much more common in horses wearing a bit than in those wearing a bitless bridle.)

Top: Shorten the reins but don't pull backward. The rein-back is actually initiated by Andrea's weight shift and the leg pressure that signals her horse to step backward.

Bottom: When your horse reacts as Fabiola does here, by stepping forward, the reins should keep him from completing the step while your legs continue to push until he has found his way backward.

Steering

As with all other exercises, a good, brisk walk is the foundation of effective steering. In our usual fashion, proceed systematically: Start with groundwork and make your horse understand what you want him to do when you apply rein aids on either side. Practice until you can precisely and subtly control him. (Revisit chapter 1, p. 1, to review.)

Once your horse understands the exercise on the ground, progress to work under saddle. At first, flex and bend him while he is standing still. This allows you to check the degree of "steering control" you already have over your horse. Flexing and bending also allows you to gently yet firmly test the flexibility of your horse's forehand. Find out how supple and flexible his neck muscles are. This form of preparation is not only about gymnasticizing your horse but also about discovering whether your horse will react to a subtle signal by yielding immediately.

If he does not want to bend, you may have made it too difficult for him to do so willingly. This often is a mental issue in horses and, thus, a question of "gymnasticizing" his mind rather than his body. If you can gently flex and bend your horse at a halt, you have established an important prerequisite for being able to tell him where to go once he is moving.

Next, practice steering at the walk before progressing to trot and canter. A platitude, you think? Our experience keeps proving the necessity of repeating this principle. We often see riders dashing through the arena in an unco-ordinated fashion at a racing trot, missing others by inches, their horse's neck as stiff as a board. "I want my horse to show some impulsion," is their reply when we ask what they are doing. What is even worse is that these riders often actually believe that their horses are moving correctly and with impulsion in these scenarios.

Canter is another matter. We've heard riders say, "I'll just let him strike off into canter," when their horse does not precisely react to other aids. As a result, the horse canters along through time and space in an uncoordinated manner, his rider a mere passenger being transported, with no signs of con-

> **Tip   Ride at a Walk**
>
> Pay lots of attention to the work you do at the walk! Perfect it and come up with creative variations of exercises at the walk before you move on to faster gaits. And just so you know—it can actually be pretty darn challenging to ride a really good walk.

trolled steering apparent.

Riding at an extended walk wakes up both horse and rider and is an extremely effective way to activate the horse's hindquarters. Gymnasticizing (suppling) the muscles in and around the haunches is an important step to organizing weight distribution in turns. In turns, the horse's inside hind leg is supposed to swing far underneath his body and carry most of the weight of his trunk, as well as that of the rider. When your horse is incapable of doing this, he uses his body the wrong way, which over time, leads to overstrain and tension.

Steering: How It Is Done

As in other exercises, the first thing you should do is come up with a plan of

Andrea demonstrates steering practice at the walk:

1 Horse and rider look in the same direction.
2 When the horse does not want to bend correctly and lets his inside shoulder fall in, your inside leg needs to apply pressure at the girth and your inside hand should lift the rein close to the horse's neck.
3 By rotating her upper body, Andrea supports her horse in the turn.

action. Please do not imagine yourself riding an entire reining pattern or dressage test as your attention span will most likely only "stay tuned" for a couple of yards. When it comes to working on steering, many riders have problems deciding on where to go. You might be thinking that your surroundings make

In turns, you need to sit straight and upright. Do not lean into a turn.

the decision for you. Although this is true to some degree, you should make it a habit to make conscious decisions about where you want your horse to go.

In a matter of moments, you should decide between left or right or straight ahead. It is not enough to be thinking, "Hmmm, let's see…" two seconds before you hit the wall of the indoor arena. You need to be aware that you will get to a point where you have to make a decision and take action. Thinking ahead and deciding on a direction helps you to ride even, smooth, and harmonious curves, turns, and other school figures because you prepare for them well in advance. A good friend of ours once said, "When we are able to determine or change the direction of the horse, we determine his future."

When you consider his history as a prey animal and the need to escape from predators, changes in direction are probably relatively important in the eyes of your horse. You, the rider, are directly influencing his immediate future. In this way, asking for a change of direction shifts a great deal of responsibility onto your shoulders. Depending on the direction, you provide your horse with a stronger feeling of security or a sense of a lack of it—and this is true whether you are aware of it or not.

Once you have decided where you want to go, focus your eyes in that direction. As a consequence, your head and your upper body will follow suit and slightly turn in the direction you aim for. Make sure your upper body rotates rather than leans to the side— leaning disturbs your horse's balance.

Slide your outside leg to its "guarding" position (see p. 55) behind the girth and apply a small amount of pres-

sure. If you are about to turn left, this should be your right leg. Your inside leg (the left in this example) remains at the girth in its basic position. If your horse tries to cut corners and drifts inside, the inside leg needs to be ready to apply pressure. Your horse should move and bend around your inside leg.

A good way to check if your horse is reacting to your weight and leg aids is to delay the use of your rein aids—see if you can turn almost without them. The reins tell the horse how much his forehand is supposed to swing into the turn. The inside rein directly determines the degree of bending while the outside rein limits it. The latter yields only enough that the horse is able to comfortably bend.

Make sure that you do not simply use the reins to pull your horse through a corner "in one stiff piece." By consciously increasing the pressure of the reins, you ask your horse to yield to them. When he obeys your request, reward him by ceasing pressure. This means you use your rein aids in intervals (see p. 37). When you are riding a particularly tight turn, you can "ask" and "yield" five to six times during the exercise in order to achieve the bend your horse needs. It goes without saying that at this stage, you should not yield all the way to a loose rein but only enough to decrease pressure and reward your horse for his good work.

The inside rein (inside the bend) must not be pulled backward but instead clearly act in a sideways manner, pointing in the direction you want to go. If your horse does not understand exactly what it is you are asking, move your hand further sideways away from his neck so you can achieve a more pronounced lateral bend.

Dr. Robert Cook's Research

British veterinarian, Robert Cook, FR-CVS, PhD, from Tufts University, Cummings School of Veterinary Medicine in Massachusetts, has spent over 50 years researching illnesses and injuries of the horse's mouth, ear, nose and throat. For most of his veterinary career, Dr. Cook has worked as a surgeon, teacher and researcher at university schools of veterinary medicine in the United Kingdom and United States. His research focus has enabled him to make a particular study of the effect of the bit on the behavior of the horse. He was shown that the cause of many serious diseases—of the digestive and respiratory systems especially—can be traced to the bit. In 1999, Dr. Cook developed his signature crossunder "Bitless Bridle" (www.bitlessbridle.com), and in 2011, at 80 years of age, he continues to publish in scientific and horse journals.

Before we continue with schooling exercises for your horse, we would like to take a closer look at Dr. Cook's research, which has uncovered many behavioral and disease problems caused by the bit.

Gag Reflex

According to Dr. Cook's research on the physiology and anatomy of the horse, a bit in the mouth triggers inappropriate digestive system responses that are in conflict with the respiratory, cardiovascular, and musculoskeletal system responses required for exercise. The cavity of the horse's mouth, with its sensitive tongue and filtering lips has evolved to admit vegetable food and liquid, nothing else. Food is first carefully selected by the lips and the horse's sense of smell, then cut and ground by the teeth, rolled around the hard palate by the body of the tongue, and mixed with saliva in the mouth. Eventually, it is passed into the throat where the root of the tongue and the soft palate forms it into a shape and substance suitable for swallowing. This critical step involves sliding semi-liquid food or water safely past the entrance to the windpipe so that it ends up in the stomach and not the lungs. The stabled horse

Whatever its material or shape, the bit is a foreign body in the horse's sensitive mouth. Riders often fail to recognize the many and varied signs of pain and distress that a bit can cause.

has to swallow a drier bolus (soft ball) of chewed hay.

All this swallowing has to be done in such a way that the horse can still breathe. The throat serves as a "switch plate" for both breathing and swallowing, and its two functions have to be carefully coordinated. This delicate dance is masterminded by two different nervous systems, but they both have to harmonize with each other for the common good. When grazing and drinking, the parasympathetic nervous system (for rest and relaxation) is the leader in the dance. When running, the sympathetic nervous system (for flight and fight) is the leader, and the dance is far more athletic.

According to Dr. Cook, a bit throws a spanner in the works and seriously upsets the program. When a bit is strapped in the mouth, the horse can neither spit it out nor swallow it. Given free choice, the horse would never have admitted the bit in the first place. Once it is installed, the horse is forced to manage two dance programs simultaneously: a slow and measured eating minuet and a fast and galloping can-can. The bit cries "chew and swallow" and the legs cry "run." The throat is bewildered. It cannot do both at the same time, and it cannot do either properly. The brain receives conflicting messages. Dr. Cook sums up the eating/breathing conflict when he writes, "Putting a bit in the mouth of a horse about to work is akin to putting a muzzle on a horse about to eat."

When the horse swallows a bolus of hay, his voice box closes off the windpipe and opens up the gullet. Under no circumstances must food go down the windpipe. Inhalation pneumonia can be fatal.

When eating, the horse breathes

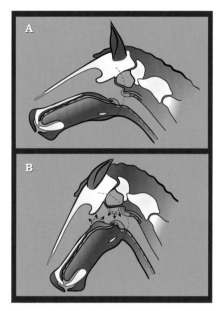

Figures A and B show what happens to the airway depending on head position.
A. The head and neck extended and airway unobstructed.
B. The head and neck flexed and airway obstructed at the level of the throat. It is bent and crimped like a badly damaged drinking straw. The soft walls of the throat tend to collapse during inhalation. The floor of the throat (the soft palate) floats up and the roof of the throat droops down. In some cases, the turbulent airflow created is enough to generate a "roaring" noise on inhalation.

slowly and gently. His need for oxygen is still present, but the demand is nothing like it is when running.

When the horse is working, his need for oxygen is urgent, all-absorbing and hugely increased. A foreign body, in his mouth and under tension, is not only painful but an impediment to breathing and a mental distraction from the job his rider is asking him to carry out.

Effects on the Tongue and Breathing Process

Dr. Cook believes that the use of a bit represents overkill. The horse is sensitive enough to feel a fly landing on his face; he does not need to be "shouted at" with a bit in order to "hear" what the rider wishes to say. The pain of a bit often makes a horse "deaf," so he cannot focus on the message anyway. In addition, poll flexion, tongue movement, jaw movement, and the need to swallow saliva, disturbs the horse in his natural way of breathing. Training techniques such as hyperflexion

("Rollkur"), where the horse's nose is far behind the vertical, exaggerate the problem.

If too much pressure is placed on a bit your horse may, either voluntarily or involuntarily, curl his head and neck into an incorrect position for breathing in order to escape or alleviate the pain. When his nose moves behind the vertical ("behind the bit") and his mouth gapes to soften the pressure, his airway becomes obstructed at the level of the

throat. Alternatively, your horse may attempt to decrease the pressure on his tongue by retracting its tip, in which case the root of the tongue bulges upward, carrying the soft palate with it and narrowing the throat airway. The root of the tongue also moves backward and in so doing partially blocks the entrance to the windpipe. The long and muscular tongue has an interesting property that it shares with a river. Restriction of its volume at any one region requires an equivalent expansion of its volume at some other region.

Sadly, horses are often unfairly punished for retracting their tongue or putting it over the bit, as well as for a vast number of other bit-induced behaviors that are, at best, inconvenient to the rider and, at worst, a hazard to the safety of both horse and rider. These bit-induced behaviors are perfectly normal evolutionary responses to pain and distress. The fault for their expression is ours. The horse should not be blamed and the behaviors should not be regarded as vices. It is our responsibility to recognize what we have done and make the necessary corrections.

Bit pain at the tip of a horse's tongue can affect the whole horse. Every metabolic process is impaired by lack of oxygen and the hyperacidity of the blood. If the horse has to spend extra energy on breathing, he has less energy for working. Performance is limited, fatigue sets in earlier, stumbling may occur, falls and catastrophic accidents may follow.

At the canter and gallop, the horse strides in time with the rhythm of his breathing—one stride for every breath. If he cannot breathe properly, he cannot stride properly. The rhythm of the gait is disturbed and performance suffers.

The working horse can best breathe

By loosening the reins a little, Andrea gives Moraleja the opportunity to stretch her head forward and "open" in the throat (and airway) if she needs to.

when allowed to stretch his head and neck. Bending the head and neck at the poll or further back can trigger a cascade of problems due to pain and a shortage of air. Too little oxygen and too much carbon dioxide has a direct and negative effect on skeletal muscle performance. While skeletal muscles are able to recover somewhat if allowed short breaks, heart muscle may suffer more severe consequences. Hearts beat unceasingly and cannot stop to take a break. A heart deprived of oxygen will take the "heart" out of the horse.

Another harmful effect of the bit is that airway obstruction increases the strength of the suction pressure that develops in the lung during inhalation. Consequently, the delicate air sacs of the lung suffer "bruising" and the end result is bleeding or EIPH (exercise-induced pulmonary hemorrhage). Though this is a problem that attracts most attention in the racehorse, it can and does occur in many other disciplines, including dressage. The effect of abnormal suction on the skin of a horse's lung is akin, in Dr. Cook's opinion, to the effect of a "hickey" on human skin. The only difference is that as the "skin" of the lung is so much more delicate, it breaks and bleeds. (Dr. Cook proposes that NPPE—Negative Pressure Pulmonary Edema—would be a better name for "bleeding" in the horse, as it describes the mechanism for its occurrence. There is a comparable problem by that name found in humans.)

Bit-Induced Bone Spurs on the Bars of the Mouth

The bars of the mouth are two knife edges of bone in the lower jaw that lie between the incisor teeth and the first cheek teeth. The gum that lightly covers the bare bone in the mouth is an in-

In this photo, you can clearly see how this horse increases his oxygen intake. He breathes through wide-open nostrils with his neck stretched slightly forward.

timate part of the bone itself. When the bit damages gum, which it does very often, it damages bone. In 2011, Dr. Cook published the results of a survey he completed of four museum collections of horse skulls on the East Coast of the United States. From 125 lower jaw specimens of domesticated horses, 78 (62 percent) showed bone spur formation. This indicates that using a bit is, in essence, the unintentional "soring" of the horse's sensitive mouth.

Tooth Damage

Dr. Cook's museum survey also showed that the bit frequently damaged the first cheek tooth in the lower jaw. In a few cases, the erosion was enough to have destroyed the tooth completely, resulting in its loss, and even to have caused an infection in the surrounding bone. From 114 teeth examined, 69 (61 percent) showed erosion. Collectively, 88 percent of the specimens showed evidence of bit damage to either the bars of the mouth or the teeth. Understandably, none of the 12 feral specimens showed either problem. Dr. Cook has

since examined 36 Pleistocene specimens (2.5 million to 12,000 years old) and they too were normal. The dental health of the undomesticated horse is, he says, an object lesson to us.

Pain-Induced Behavior

Dr. Cook describes a host of behavioral problems he attributes to bit use in horses. He shows that bit-induced deviations of behavior are often problems that relate not just to the head but to the whole of the horse. Some problems arise suddenly, whereas others develop gradually and insidiously. Many are problems that have never previously been recognized as being caused by the bit. Many behaviors are specific to the bit and others are behaviors that may also be caused by pain elsewhere, for example in the back and even in the foot. The following is only a partial listing of Dr. Cook's "blacklist" of bit-related behavior:

> Postures commonly regarded as incorrect headsets, including "behind the bit," "leaning on the bit," "against the bit," and "above the bit."
> "Tongue problems," such as tongue lolling, tongue retraction, and putting the tongue over the bit.
> Open or gaping mouth (if the mouth isn't already bound shut with a tight noseband or flash!)
> Constant movement of the lower jaw and/or tongue.
> Hyperflexion with no activity in the hindquarters (they "trail" behind).
> Dropped and/or stiff back.
> Biting down or "clamping" on the bit ("getting the bit between the teeth").
> Abnormal breathing sounds when the horse is asked to collect.
> Resistance during tacking-up (particularly when putting on the bridle).
> General insubordination (poor or

surly behavior during groundwork and handling, as well as riding).

Even though the above very small sample of "blacklist" bit behaviors are primarily caused by pain, the following factors may also play a supporting role:

> Lack of exercise; poorly fitting equipment; inappropriate living conditions ("solitary confinement," lack of turnout, lack of light/fresh air, boredom); unbalanced diet; and improper training (excessive mental and physical demands, rough handling).

Long ago, the great riding masters, such as Xenophon, pointed out the dangers of the bit and the extreme pain a rider can cause his horse, intentionally or unintentionally. Almost every book on tack, the aids, and on riding in general (irrespective of riding style) warns riders of the harm a bit can cause. When a standard method or tradition of management does more harm than good, does it make sense to continue using it or should we look for a better alternative?

Fritz Stahlecker, a famous German dressage trainer, known for his work with horses in-hand, is very outspoken on this subject: "If many people have been doing the same thing for generations, something may be wrong!" Those who swim against the current and are prepared to take a fresh and critical look at our traditional methods will make interesting discoveries.

More Reasons to Consider Bitless Riding

Many of the "problems" we encounter when riding bitted horses can be solved by removing the bit and training the horse in a pain-free manner. Without a bit, it is possible to reduce the risk of riding, ride more correctly, ride in a way that is more beneficial to your horse's health, and give yourself and your horse more pleasure. Your horse will develop a stronger back, be better balanced emotionally, happier in his work, and more compliant in mind and body. We maintain that this applies to riding anywhere—indoor and outdoor arenas, as well as on the trail and in competition. It is possible to teach your horse the most difficult of movements—whether dressage or any other discipline—without using a bit. The horse is perfectly capable of executing them just as correctly, and perhaps more correctly, than he would wearing a bit.

Think about it: The highlight of many an expo or clinic is when a rider takes off his horse's tack, and performs difficult exercises with perfection. Difficult exercises, whether English or Western, are demanding of our riding skills. They are not dependent on our equipment. It is first and foremost our riding abilities that are crucial to our success. We should always consider the possibility that our equipment could be an impediment.

With this in mind, and considering the many problems the "average" rider encounters with a bitted horse, use of a crossunder bitless bridle can solve many of these problems. As it is possible for you and your horse to work together without a bit in a "kinder" way, why not just drop the bit completely?

Of course, there are horses that do not appear to have any problems wearing a bit. Nevertheless, we advise their riders to take a careful look at Dr. Cook's observations (beginning on p. 64) regarding the cascade of problems triggered by a foreign body in a horse's

Top: While wearing a crossunder bitless bridle and carrying his nose slightly in front of the vertical, this horse can breathe freely.

Middle: This horse shows a lovely topline with the perfect amount of "positive" tension. The neck ring allows him to carry his head freely (see more about riding with a neck ring starting on p. 76).

Bottom: While riding a large circle, this young rider demonstrates how you can bend your horse correctly with a crossunder bitless bridle.

Left: Shiva is a well-trained Haflinger mare who knows how to handle a bit.

Right: Smiley is much more relaxed wearing a bitless bridle.

mouth. A horse can only be confirmed with any certainty as being happy with a bit if his behavior does not improve when the bit is removed.

Bit Pressure

Experiments (performed by very different parties) have shown that the pressure the reins and bit produce within the horse's mouth is extremely high—yet another argument against using a bit. The tongue, especially, is exposed to many pounds of pressure. What is more disturbing according to these studies is the fact that even "the most sensitive hands" cause massive effects in the horse's mouth. After all, it is not about whether a rider has sensitive or rough hands, but about the physical transmission of energy by way of equipment.

Less Space

Studies by the University of Veterinary Medicine in Hanover, Germany, have shown that there is much less space for a bit within the horse's mouth than previously thought. A bit always touches the tongue and palate and is thus constantly in contact with the oral mu-

cosa. The danger of involuntarily but continually causing small trauma is, therefore, relatively great.

As a logical result, we can conclude that the absence of a metal object from the horse's mouth is much gentler on this highly sensitive area.

"De-Stressing" Horses

We often notice that when switching from using a bit to a bitless bridle, most horses become calmer, more relaxed, and more mentally balanced. Despite the many other factors that influence the horse's mental state (living conditions, diet, exercise, prior experience, handling, training), the changes noticeable after switching to a bitless bridle are significant.

Unfortunately, we have to deal with many abused horses who have every reason not to trust humans, who have shut down mentally, show all sorts of resistance and actively defend themselves. Is it not amazing that allegedly problematic horses are easier to handle once you decrease your physical control over them? For example, it is possible to soften a so-called "hard-mouthed" horse (that is presumably difficult to control because he ignores the rein aids) so he responds to the aids by using a bitless bridle. Being hard-mouthed is a trait a horse acquires because of a rider with unyielding or rough hands.

Starting Horses under Saddle

Originally, bitless bridles were used to school young, inexperienced riding horses. Bitless bridles have proven quite useful to treat the young mouth with care, and to familiarize the green horse with the weight of a rider first, training and controlling him mainly through seat and leg aids. Once the horse knows and obeys the aids and is used to carrying weight, then a bit is commonly placed in his mouth. He can continue to wear the bitless bridle at the same time so the bit remains untouched at first and only gradually gains in importance as the trainer increases rein contact.

In addition, when a young horse's permanent teeth are erupting (which often coincides with starting him under saddle), using a bitless bridle, even temporarily, can be very useful and prevent defensive reactions in the horse.

Beginners and Children

Practice in the saddle and generally improving your body awareness are the only means to developing a balanced posture without a dependence on the reins. This is the prerequisite for keeping your hands still, sensitive, and controlled. For this reason, beginners should not use reins that are directly attached to a bit. The same applies to children who are mostly interested in having fun on horseback—they do best with a bitless bridle. Especially for beginners and children, a well-trained horse ridden with a bitless bridle is the perfect teacher.

The use of a bitless bridle and/or neck ring (see p. 76) makes lessons at beginner level even more efficient as students focus less on the reins and more on the rest of their body. In this way, they develop an independent seat, better balance and body awareness, as well as a feeling for weight and leg aids, more quickly. They also gain a better understanding of the purpose and use of focus and breathing when on horseback.

Left: It has been easier for Moraleja to leave her negative experience with riding behind since Andrea has used a bitless bridle, with which Andrea can be firm but always gentle.

Right: Shiva, who we mentioned works well with a bit in her mouth on p. 70, is also a dependable partner when wearing a bitless bridle.

Earlier in this book we shared our basic principle of "As little as possible and no more than necessary." This leads us to the eventual fun and freedom offered of working with your horse in a neck ring.

When you use the fewest and subtlest aids possible and know how to apply them correctly, you can create a form of freedom both you and your horse can enjoy. Riding with a neck ring is a real piece of that freedom!

Almost "Naked"

The content of this book can be understood in many different ways. On the one hand, we aim to grant our horses as much freedom as possible. On the other, the degree of freedom must always be at a level that ensures the safety of both horse and rider.

Misty-eyed romanticized "freedom" in the sense of antiauthoritarian training that allows the horse to do whatever he wants has nothing to do with what we have in mind.

In comparison to your horse, your physique is rather delicate. Therefore, you can only grant your horse some "freedom"—it must be in concert with established boundaries and rules of conduct. If you succeed at the balancing act between respect and trust, two inseparable aspects of horsemanship in our estimation, then finding different kinds of freedom with your horse is both possible and safe.

Riding without saddle or bit—a piece of cake, isn't it?

Many riders imagine a "feeling of freedom and adventure" when they think about horses. This is also the dream that often inspires people to take up riding in the first place. Flying over vast plains in unison and harmony with a horse, without saddle or bridle, feeling the wind in their face, the movement of their horse underneath them, and (in the dream) knowing that at the subtlest cue, the horse will come to a smooth and gentle stop ...

Unfortunately, such dreams usually burst when beginners are confronted with reality: Everyday riding life at lesson barns and in riding schools looks completely different!

We actually believe that "Riding Free" not only applies to your horse, but also to you: Free yourself from the constraints, burdens, and stresses of your daily routine and concentrate only on the friend and partner that is carrying you. Free yourself from prejudices, fears, and habits. This requires courage! But, "If you have the courage to leave your old world behind, you will discover a new one!"

When you can "become one" with your horse and learn what it means to "feel," pictures like these become possible. The most important thing is that you must trust one another so it becomes less and less significant whether you are holding reins, mane, or nothing at all in your hands when you are riding.

Markus is able to grant his horse the highest degree of freedom because he knows his horse will listen to him and obey him.

Neck Ring Riding for Beginners

At our riding school, riding with a neck ring—made of lariat rope and adjustable in size; you can get one at www.ttouch.com—is a part of "normal" lessons. With the well-trained horses we have, this is pure delight for all involved.

As soon as our beginner riders have established a basic degree of balance and coordination, we introduce them to riding with a neck ring. We consider this a valuable diversion for horse and rider. We also encourage our students to cool down their horses using a neck ring, and for the more advanced riders, we build a small jumping course to be mastered in a playful yet precise manner.

Initially, we teach using the neck ring in an enclosed outdoor ring or indoor arena. The rider must first learn how to gain sufficient control over his or her body. The advantage of integrating the neck ring into the training of beginners is that they learn right from the start how to establish their balance, to sit in a relaxed manner on the horse's back, and to apply correct weight and leg aids. With a neck ring, you cannot compensate for an incorrect posture or seat by simply holding on to the reins. One-on-one lessons in small groups and paying attention to the needs of individual horse and rider teams help expand each rider's limits step by step.

In addition to the pedagogic value of this approach, we can fulfill, to some degree, that rider dream of boundless freedom discussed at the beginning of this chapter.

Do you think this is all a bit silly or "out there" for serious riders and trainers? Well, what was it that first brought you to horses and riding? We feel that

In order to ride bareback with only a neck ring, you first need to develop a good deal of balance and feeling on the horse's back.

"Self-carriage" comes in many forms. Here, at the walk and for just a moment, Fabiola stretches her neck and poll as much as she can.

living your dreams, experiencing enthusiasm and pure joy, and perceiving the world with all your senses are also an important part of riding, whatever your ambitions in the saddle.

Self-Carriage instead of Contact

When you are working with a neck ring, your goal is not to establish contact in the classical sense but for you and your horse to develop a higher degree of autonomy and responsibility concerning balance and surefootedness. If you have gymnasticized your horse well under saddle (see p. 41), using a neck ring will encourage him to display a degree of self-carriage that reflects his level of training.

Preparing with Groundwork

The prerequisite for the safe use of a neck ring is, once again, thorough preparation on the ground. This is when you explain to your horse how you expect him to react to the neck ring, since the aids are applied differently from a common bridle. The aids affect other parts of the horse's body: Instead of head, poll, nose, and mouth, you work with the neck and throat. The nature of the tactile stimuli is different as well: The neck ring creates short impulses issued in intervals and the energy produced is more "pressure" than "pull."

Once your horse has learned to yield to the slightest cues from the neck ring, in every direction, on the ground, you can start practicing under saddle. He should react to the aids applied by the neck ring in the same way he did during groundwork.

Exercises

Halt-Walk
In order to ask your horse to transition from halt to walk, hold the neck ring in your hand(s) so it hardly touches your horse's neck at all. Hold the ring passively and in a relaxed manner.

In-hand preparation: Initially, Markus practices halt and bending when cued by the neck ring from the ground. To ensure safety, start your neck ring training session in the round pen or indoor arena.

Sit upright and relaxed as you apply the usual aids (legs and forward-driving seat aid) to ask your horse to start walking forward (see p. 54). Make sure that your horse learns right away to walk at briskly, with energy.

If your horse reacts to your forward-driving aids, reduce them immediately to let him know he did the right thing—as you have done with every other exercise so far. Remember to resume for-ward-driving aids only if necessary. When you work with a neck ring, your body (focus, breathing, legs, and weight) becomes all the more important since you no longer have the horse's head and/or mouth as an additional receptor of your aids.

Once your horse moves at a brisk walk forward as requested and your aids turn passive (serving a "guarding" or "observing" function), allow your horse to move as freely as possible, but remain ready to encourage him with aids if necessary.

Halt

Even with what might seem like little means to physically control your horse, it should not be a problem at all to transition to halt using the neck ring.

Apply your halt aids (except the reins) as usual: Decide on a point at which you want your horse to halt, breathe out, sink deep into the saddle, and lower your heels slightly toward the ground.

Place the neck ring around the middle of your horse's neck and apply the following aids until you get the desired reaction: ask (apply slight pressure to the neck), yield, repeat. To most horses, this form of aid is very logical and they react correctly at the first attempt—as if they had been ridden with a neck ring for weeks! It is also quite amazing how easily most horses adopt a very

nice frame in the neck ring. They lower their head and round their back. It should be noted, however, that the neck ring is also a very helpful tool to encourage horses with deep-set necks to show some elevation.

If your horse does not immediately react to your halt aids, place the neck ring a little higher up the neck, closer to the throat, and repeat. Some horses find it easier to understand your intentions this way. You must, however, be careful and gentle when using a neck ring near the throat—avoid jerky movements at all costs. And be aware that with a neck ring, you cannot "force" your horse to stop! Repeat your pressure "impulses"; do not attempt forceful pulling or yanking.

If at first you experience problems using the neck ring, combine it with your usual bridle of choice. Practice the exercises described earlier in this book and make sure that you can really stop your horse precisely and with light aids

It is okay if it takes this mare a few steps to transition to a halt. With the neck ring, Markus applies pressure "impulses" to the middle of her neck. He also uses his weight, breathing, and legs to fulfill their end of the deal.

with a bridle. If you discover that your aids do not seem to be working and must be stronger than you feel should really be necessary, work first to improve your halts and steering with a bridle before trying a neck ring! The better your horse reacts to your rein aids, the quicker a neck ring can actively replace them.

Advanced riders and those who find that the walk-halt transition to come easily can try extensions and collection within the gait. Ask your horse to lengthen his strides before effortlessly getting him to shorten them by applying light impulses with ther neck ring. The ultimate challenge is to eventually softly transition from trot to halt with a minimum of aids.

Riding Turns

As in other exercises, riding turns depends very much on the interplay of all the aids. How you use your body to apply these aids and how well you mentally prepare for the exercise are integral to leading your horse into a turn smoothly.

Your outside hand (outside the bend) must apply the neck ring to the respective side of the horse's neck. The command is easiest for your horse to understand when you place the neck ring around the upper part of his neck. If he is very sensitive, it might suffice to simply tilt the ring in the direction of the turn so that, on the inside of the turn, it is closer to his shoulder and on the outside of the turn, closer to his head. In this way, the neck ring determines exactly the degree of lateral neck flexion your horse needs during the turn.

Applying the neck ring to the side of your horse's neck that is outside the bend is similar to the concept of neck reining in Western riding. In neck reining, the rein aid equals slight pressure or a soft touch, acting on the horse's neck.

If, during introductory groundwork

Fabiola comes to a good (almost) square halt without tension in horse or rider.

you taught your horse to yield instantly and willingly to the slightest amount of pressure, he will easily understand that application of the neck ring in these ways is the command to move sideways.

Initially, again use the neck ring in combination with your bridle when starting to practice steering under saddle. When schooling a turn to the left, for example, combine applying the neck ring to the right side of your horse's neck with a gentle "asking" rein aid on the left inside rein. Progressively reduce the amount of rein aid in favor of the neck ring. Note: It is important to make sure that your horse bends correctly when using a neck ring. In order to do this, apply precise leg aids. If your horse continuously drops his inside shoulder with the neck ring, you can touch the respective shoulder with a crop as a reminder.

Rein-Back

The best and easiest way to school rein-back with a neck ring is to properly teach your horse the exercise with a bridle first (see p. 58). He should learn to step backward with a rounded back and without throwing his head in the air. Lean forward just a little to help your horse by taking some of your weight off of his hindquarters ("making" yourself a little lighter). Use your forward-driving leg aids to ask him to step backward. The goal is for your horse to learn to react to the shifting of your weight so that contact with the neck ring is only necessary as a "guarding" aid when you apply the forward-driving leg aids. If your horse does not immediately understand, apply short light impulses with the neck ring.

Left Page: Two cones are very helpful optical aids when you want to school figure eights and practice steering with the neck ring. Markus is looking at the cones and thus shifting his weight in the correct direction for the turn.

Left and Below: In order to ask his horse to back up, Markus applies the neck ring to the upper part of the horse's neck and shifts his weight slightly forward. Intermittent pressure on the neck ring is applied if necessary.

A length of thin rope, looped around the neck as shown here, can be used instead of a neck ring.

Maximizing the Sensitivity of Horse and Rider

When working with a neck ring, you must focus your attention on different aspects of riding than you do when using a bridle. As a consequence, it is very likely that your posture and seat will automatically improve since you have to use your seat and body to apply all the aids. As you only have a minimum of rein aids at your disposal, your body needs to "talk" to your horse more precisely.

If you depended on the reins before working with a neck ring, be prepared to have this dependence exposed—but also improved. Furthermore, riding without a bridle trains you to sense when and how strongly to apply your aids. Many horses show sensitive reactions to the reduction of rein signals. For example, when first ridden in a neck ring, we often see them eagerly stretching their neck forward and down.

What is even more interesting is the reaction of the advanced rider who suddenly finds herself riding without reins. How would you react if we told you that we are about to take off your horse's bridle and replace it with a simple loop of rope—and that we expect you to ride (and ride well) that way? The rider's face reflects many different emotions at this point: anything from skepticism, doubt, incredulity, and tense expectation to utter joy and elation.

Advanced riders are often much more impressed by the neck ring experience than beginners, quite simply because they are familiar with the aids used to control and direct the horse, and know how to use them, and how strong they sometimes seem to need to be. We find that English riders, especially, who are used to riding with constant contact, find it difficult to "let go" and to consciously drop the reins. They feel helpless—until they realize how sensitively their horse is reacting to their seat and leg aids...without the reins!

During our lessons and through spe-

Top and middle: When riding with a thin rope instead of a neck ring, Markus holds his hands as if he were holding reins.

cific exercises, we help our students overcome fear and tension when riding without a bridle. They learn to "let go" and discover a new form of body awareness. As their self-confidence improves, they develop a more acute feeling for subtle, well-measured aids, and as a result, they are more likely to trust in their horse.

Bottom: Here are two versions of the same turn. In the picture on the left, Markus visibly applies the neck ring to the side of the horse's neck while rotating his upper body in the direction of the turn. In the picture on the right, you see the same exercise with refined aids.

Equipment

There are no fixed rules when riding with a neck ring. The ring itself comes in many forms, among them the one designed and made famous by Linda Tellington-Jones that we mentioned at the beginning of this chapter: a stiff, adjustable ring made of lariat rope (www.ttouch.com). As explained on the previous page, you can also use any thin, sturdy rope, a simple lead rope, or even a hula hoop!

You can hold the neck ring with one or both hands. We recommend first using it in combination with a bridle, and over time reducing your rein aids until all you need to do is touch your horse

with the neck ring in a way similar to the neck-reining technique used in Western riding (see more about this on p. 81). The aids other than your rein aids (voice, breathing, focus, weight, and legs) become very important.

In summary:

> During moments when you do not need the neck ring because your horse is doing what you have asked him to do, hold it in your hands so it does not touch his neck.

> In order to steer, stop, or back up, apply short "impulses" (pressure) on his neck in intervals. Do not pull or jerk (especially in the throat area). Constant pulling on the ring quickly desensitizes your horse to it, which is undesirable when you intend to ride with it in place of your rein aids.

> With practice, you can school advanced exercises, such as turn on the forehand or haunches, shoulder-in, and lateral movements.

> If necessary, you can use a crop when schooling the neck ring aids. Apply it in a conscientious manner to the respective shoulder.

Perfect harmony between Markus and Fabiola in a turn.

> ### Tip   Keep in Shape
>
> We ask our students to obey the following rule: "When using the neck ring, make sure it always maintains its original circular form." This way, we give our students a visual cue to help them from pulling on the ring and/or using too much force.

"Riding free" is fun! Markus and Fabiola are a great team.

Riding Bareback

The dream of riding without saddle and bridle can come true—and more easily than you might think! Riders of all styles and disciplines should ride bareback on a regular basis. In the same way as working with a neck ring, bareback riding forces you to improve any riding weaknesses. Your seat, balance, and coordination will improve.

Mounting

Regardless of whether we ride with or without a saddle, mounting is always an issue—that is, how do we get on without causing our horse discomfort? Unfortunately, when we mount, the horse's balance is always disturbed for a moment. Even experienced riders who can get on swiftly and quickly have their body weight on only one side of the horse for a brief period of time.

We teach our students to get on and off their horse on both sides, whether they are using a saddle or riding bareback. In fact, in many of the daily tasks around horses, we make sure to divide our time evenly between the left and

A lovely trot in a nice frame without saddle or bridle.

When first mounting your horse bareback, have an assistant hold your horse and use a mounting block.

right sides, including:
> Putting on and taking off a halter
> Saddling
> Mounting
> Dismounting
> And, of particular importance, leading the horse

In this way, we school ambidexterity, which is one of the goals of horse training, we support the horse in developing balanced body awareness, and we also benefit by improving our own coordination. It also takes into consideration the fact that the horse's back is exposed to a significant degree of strain when we always mount from the same side, which can have negative long-term effects. This is unnecessary and can easily be prevented by regularly switching sides when getting on.

You can reduce the chance of one-sided strain even more if you always use a mounting block. Riders often feel self-conscious or as if they aren't athletic when they get on their horse from an elevated position. We, however, consider a mounting block very sensible since

---

Tip | Careful Dismounting

Dismounting can be dangerous when you use the stirrups the way you do while mounting—that is, one foot on the ground, the other still in the stirrup. If this is the moment your horse decides to move, your foot can easily get stuck in the stirrup, you might lose your balance, and if your horse is scared by this unanticipated turn of events, you can end up being dragged behind him! Prevent accidents like this by removing both feet from the stirrups first, then slowly lowering your body down your horse's side.

---

it helps protect the horse's back. Even with a block, be sure to alternate sides. When a block isn't available, you can use a set of stable folding steps, a stair, a low wall, or—when out on a trail ride—a small boulder or tree stump. Your horse will be grateful for it.

Using a Mounting Block
When using a movable mounting block, such as a set of folding steps, to get on your horse while using a saddle, position yourself close to your horse. The better your horse is used to standing still while you mount, the better off you will be (see p. 53). Otherwise, ask a friend to assist you and hold the horse's head.

Position the mounting block slightly behind the stirrup (which you should have adjusted in advance). Make sure the block is level and stable so it will not tip over. Step on the mounting block, place one foot in the stirrup, and mount in the usual fashion. Hold the reins in one hand and look in the direction your horse will move once you are on board. This way, you can react immediately if your horse decides to move before you are ready.

Get your horse accustomed to being led up to and standing close to stable, immovable objects like low walls, fences, and steps, and mount him with a saddle first. Always make sure there are no sharp edges or ledges that could possibly injure you or your horse.

When riding bareback, a high mounting block is very helpful. Depending on the height of your horse, you might even be able to just slide over onto his back. (Note: As mentioned before, it is very important to always make sure that the ground is level and your mounting block—whatever it may be—cannot tip over.) Before mounting a horse without a saddle, he should have learned to stand still. Review the lesson on p. 53 if necessary. When a horse moves when you are trying to mount him bareback, his slippery hair can cause use to lose your balance.

"Park" your horse close to an object you can mount from while keeping the reins in one hand. Get your horse's full attention by saying his name, for example, and briefly stroke his back with your free hand. Stand facing in the same direction as your horse, lift your leg, and gently slide over onto his back. Only after you have positioned yourself slightly behind the withers and adjusted your clothes and reins should you give your horse the command to step forward.

If you cannot find a mounting block high enough to allow you to just "glide" over onto your horse's back, it comes in handy to be physically flexible. With your horse next to the block, support yourself on his withers, spread your legs, and push yourself up onto his back, then swing your leg over. This slightly more "spirited" way of mounting should not unsettle your horse and he should remain still as before.

Mounting with an Assistant

When a mounting block is not available and you need to mount your horse bareback, an instructor or riding friend can assist you. The person helping you up should be sure that he does so in a way that will not injure his back—with his back straight and using his legs.

Stand facing your horse's torso and bend your knee at a 90-degree angle. Your mounting assistant takes a hold of your lower leg and, on the count of three, lifts you up while you push your-

self off the ground. Coordinating the motion sequence of the "leg up" takes some practice.

Tip | Ambidexterity

In order to school ambidexterity in horse and rider, we recommend mounting and dismounting on both sides. One way we teach our students to dismount when riding bareback is to swing one leg over the horse's neck so you end up sitting sideways before pushing yourself forward and landing on both feet next to your horse. This more athletic variation of the classic dismount gives you the advantage of seeing where you will land.

Mounting "Indian Style"

The "coolest" and probably most athletic way to mount a horse bareback requires some practice. We recommend practicing this method on an "inanimate" object first: a wooden fence of "horse" that will be extremely patient and will not complain about your many failed attempts ...

The biggest mistake we see riders make when riding bareback is trying to literally jump onto the horse, which requires a great amount of strength and effort. Our version of getting you up there is a form of swinging yourself up that propels you right into a riding position.

Position yourself close to one of your horse's front legs, and stand sideways facing toward his rear. With the hand closest to your horse, hold the reins and support yourself on the withers. The reins should not be tight. Swing your outside leg back in order to build momentum before swinging it up and

Top: For the leg up, hold the reins in one hand, your leg at at 90-degree angle, and have your assistant assume position— and then, go!

Bottom: Mounting with an assistant is no problem for Fabiola. She does not move a muscle.

A patient, adequately sized horse is perfect for practicing this method of mounting bareback.

over your horse's back, allowing your body to follow. Your upper body should be bent forward as much as possible during the movement, which means you must use the hand on the withers to push yourself into an upright position once you are on. Please let us repeat: This method of mounting does not involve "jumping up" from the ground but building momentum.

Info   Native Americans

Did you know that Native Americans did not strictly ride bareback? For the most part, they had their children herd their horses so that equestrian skills were perfected from a very young age and they learned the art of riding bareback early on. However, Native Americans definitely recognized the advantages a saddle provided with regard to hunting, fighting, and transportation. They used the equipment brought by Spanish explorers or adapted it to fit their needs.

Swift and agile, Markus swings his leg over Smiley's back and sits upright in the riding position.

Top right: Your legs should hang down your horse's sides in a relaxed manner.

Top left: Markus has found the correct bareback riding position.

Middle: Markus demonstrates sitting too far back.

Bottom: Here he is positioned too close to the withers.

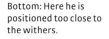

The Seat

The correct bareback riding position is slightly behind the withers, far enough back to allow you to be flexible in your pelvis and to follow your horse's movements without painful surprises!

Place your legs behind your horse's shoulders, the inside of your knees resting against his body. When riding bareback, it is important to be balanced—do not pinch with your lower legs to stay on the horse. Ask your instructor or a riding friend to hold your horse, close your eyes, and take a few deep breaths. Feel where your seat is touching your horse's body. How large or small does your seat, or the contact surface, feel to you? Do you sense the same amount of pressure on both seat bones? Do both legs feel like they are the same length? Do your toes point inward or outward? Does your seat feel different when you breathe out slowly? Mindfulness exercises like these help you develop an awareness of your body on horseback and improve your balance.

We recommend a lightly "activated" seat—that is, you do not simply sit completely relaxed and passive but instead

Top left: This is what it looks like when we lose our balance.

Top right: It is very helpful to consciously practice the counter-movement to the loss of balance, as Andrea is here.

Bottom: When she grabs the mane, Andrea is sure to keep hold of the reins at the same time.

maintain your balance with the help of minimally flexed muscles. These "activated" muscles allow you to sit symmetrically on both buttocks and the triangular base made up of the seat bones and pubic arch. This form of active muscle flexion should neither be exhausting nor should you develop "negative" tension in your body and become stiff. You will be able to sit relaxed and balanced even on the slippery bare back of the horse!

When riding bareback, we prefer to use a bitless bridle (or a halter, even) since we are prone to reflexively hold on to the reins when we get insecure or start to slide sideways. Special reflex exercises, like those we did on pp. 24 and 26, can help you maintain your posture and grab mane when your horse trips. As in other cases, initial practice of holding the reins while grabbing mane should happen on the ground. Make sure you do not let go of the reins.

Bareback riding teaches you to appreciate close, direct contact with your horse: You will feel his movements and working muscles much more clearly than when you are sitting in a saddle.

Exercise to improve rhythm: With her eyes closed, Andrea taps her thigh along with the rhythm of the striding of her horse's right front leg.

You experience firsthand the effects of your aids, particularly your weight and leg aids. Bareback, it is easier to find out how to follow your horse's movements with your seat.

In this book, we have included specific exercises that teach you an easy and safe way to do this. Horses often react even more sensitively to their riders' aids when the cushioning layer (the saddle) is removed.

First Steps

We like to start with awareness and relaxation exercises. Initial practice should occur while your horse is standing still. You might want to ask a friend to hold your horse. When you feel safe at a halt, your assistant can lead you while you hold the reins to make sure you feel a sense of control over your horse.

For beginners the first time out, a few minutes of bareback riding is enough. The unfamiliar muscle flexion and demand for good balancing skills will quickly tire out their body, which leads to "negative" tension in the rider and, consequently, in the horse.

It should also be noted that it makes little sense to completely abstain from using a saddle or at least some form of cushioning, such as a bareback pad or blanket. These pieces of equipment distribute your weight broadly and evenly, which otherwise causes spikes of pressure on certain points of your horse's back. Be aware that riding bareback for hours is not necessarily horse-friendly or gentle: Your seat bones can absolutely leave pressure marks. Bareback riding should be used as an exercise to improve your riding, your communication with your horse, and to lend variety to your training. It should supplement riding activities using a saddle or bareback pad.

When riding bareback, it is easier to feel which parts of your seat are in contact with your horse.

Slow Trot (Jog)

Asking your horse to trot very slowly (jog) allows you to follow his movement with your pelvis in a rhythmic and relaxed manner. Since the motion is slow and hardly bouncy, it is possible to ride sitting trot well without a saddle. This makes it easier for you to concentrate on the rhythm of your horse's movements and learn how to follow them with your pelvis. As a result, the entire motion will feel "round"—you are not disturbing your horse or bumping along on his back.

When you are unable to follow the horse's rhythm, however, you will consequently lag behind him. This will turn the trot into a bumpy ride: You move in opposition to your horse—that is, his back swings upward when you are on your way down, and vice versa. To both horse and rider, this becomes very uncomfortable, very quickly and leads to a loss of balance, especially when you are riding bareback.

Bareback riding at a slow trot or jog should look as effortless as in these two pictures.

More advanced riders, are probably able to find their way "back into" the rhythm of the horse's gait, whatever speed they are traveling, but we tell beginners to transition to the next-lowest gait as quickly as possible to prevent sliding around or falling off. Quick yet smooth transitions (never jerky) are very helpful in situations like this, and that is one reason why they should be practiced frequently both on the ground and in the saddle.

When you want to trot faster, it is best to relieve your horse's back a little. The forward seat and posting trot are quite strenuous exercises when riding bareback and really strain the muscles on the inside of your thighs. Moreover, it is not exactly feasible to assume either position without the help of stirrups since you shouldn't pinch with your lower legs. Nonetheless, practice in both the forward seat and the posting trot for short periods.

Horses of many breeds and sizes can enjoy bareback riding.

Canter

When riding bareback, the soft, smooth motion of canter is much more comfortable than a brisk trot. However, you need to have developed a stable, balanced seat and a "feel" for the motion sequence of canter before you try it bareback. Since you and your horse are moving at a considerably higher speed, this exercise might take some courage in the beginning. But rest assured that it is fantastic to feel the horse's powerful muscles working underneath you and to almost fly along as one!

For Advanced Riders

If you are an advanced rider, you have a little more freedom to experiment when riding bareback. You should be able to ride bareback in forward seat, posting trot, and at the canter.

At our stable, we take our advanced students out to the "playground": A large, fenced pasture featuring miscellaneous jumps, dips, hills, and bottlenecks that invite riders and their horses to have a little fun. Under professional instruction, the "playground" can be turned into a series of meaningful exercises, offering variety, diversion, and challenge for horse and rider!

Short trail rides can be very appealing, offering the possibility to become more familiar with natural obstacles, uneven terrain, or even small jumps. Remember, keep trail rides short or walk next to your horse part of the way so as not to harm his back through the localized pressure points under your seat bones (see p. 98).

Conclusion

After riding bareback or with a saddle, get in the habit of palpating your horse's back to look for potential tension or

It is a real source of joy to be able to include canter in your bareback riding session. Here Markus and Fabiola enjoy each other with nothing but a neck ring between them.

soreness. Then:

> Give him a short massage, working in long, strong strokes on both sides of the spine. If you notice sensitive areas on your horse's back, keep an eye on them over the next couple of days, check your pad or saddle for fit, and if necessary, ask a professional to have a look at it.

> Do a few "back lifts": Stand beside him facing his barrel, and place your fingers under his belly along his midline. Apply pressure until you see his topline rise. Then release, and repeat.

> Stretch your horse out: We like to feed our horses treats from the ground, inviting them to stretch their back as they reach forward-downward with their neck.

These post-workout exercises can be done after every training session. They are a form of active relaxation for your horse.

Markus and Fabiola,
having a laugh!

Useful Information

Contact Andrea and Markus Eschbach:

Eschbach Horsemanship
www.eschbach-horsemanship.com
www.bitless-riding.com
info@eschbach-horsemanship.com

Riding and Training Quick-Reference Checklists

General Rules of Training

> Plan ahead
> Have a goal
> Understand your "tools": techniques, auxiliary aids
> Create a timeline
> Acquire a knowledge of horse behavior
> Perfect aid "dosage" and timing: "The art of small steps"
> Be prepared to change training plans and adapt
> Review your performance

Skills Every Rider Must Master

In order to create a harmonious and safe relationship with your horse, you need to have the following skills:

> Stable, balanced, and rein-independent seat
> Sense for horse and motion, increasing your body awareness
> Ability to "read" your horse's behavior
> Gentle, yielding, dynamically stable rein contact
> Aid application with a minimum of energy expenditure
> Practiced reflexes (yielding)

> Perfectly measured aids and perfect timing
> Above-average concentration
> Mental stability: patience, self-control, relaxation, positive attitude
> Emotional control
> Knowledge of and understanding of the horse
> Realistic self-assessment
> Knowledge of human nature
> Knowledge of training options and techniques

Skills Every Horse Must Master

With regard to riding and handling we expect the following:
> Focused attention on the rider
> Immediate (obedient) reactions to the rider's aids
> Immediate (obedient) reactions to the subtlest of signals
> Ability to wait for signals from the rider
> Relaxed yet attentive
> Motivated to do almost anything
> Vertical and lateral flexion in poll and body (supple)
> Smooth reactions to aids

You Can Advance the Level of Training When:

> The horse reacts to the subtlest aids and commands
> You can apply aids subtly and effortlessly
> The horse reacts correctly within 1 to 3 seconds
> The horse reacts willingly, smoothly, and free of stress
> The horse gives you his (almost) undivided attention
> Desired reactions are repeatable any time, any place

What to Do When You Have a Problem:

> Self-analysis
> Situation analysis
> Go one step back
> Systematically check the basic building blocks of training
> Look for "sources of error"
> Start over from scratch
> Adapt goals, steps, and pace of training to your horse's needs
> Review performance

Types of Bitless Bridles

Some of the bitless bridles presented here we have used and thus know them well. In those cases, we provided a short description and advantages/disadvantages.

Bitless Bridle™

This bridle designed by Dr. Robert Cook (see p. 64) is based on a halter. The reins run over the poll, cross underneath the lower jaw, and run through rings attached to the sides of the noseband. Rein aids affect the horse's nose, lower jaw, cheeks, and poll. Dr. Cook's Bitless Bridle allows for correct flexing and bending, both vertically and laterally (www.bitlessbridle.com).

Bosal

The bosal—also known as a classical, manual, or Californian hackamore—has a noseband usually made of braided rawhide. Attached to it is the mecate, which acts as chin strap, reins, and lead rope and is usually made of artfully braided and knotted horsehair. The bosal is supposed to fit loosely around the horse's head. It knocks against the nose and chin where it delivers pressure "impulses." Aids can also be given by using the mecate to apply pressure against one side of the horse's neck. Traditionally, the bosal was used during the basic training of a young horse before bitting prior to schooling advanced exercises.

Simple Leather Bosal

This is a loose-fitting bridle perfectly appropriate for trail rides when used on well-trained horses. Naturally, an independent seat as well as well-developed weight and leg aids should come first. Rein aids are applied as they are when neck reining. As a consequence, correcting your horse's posture/frame can be difficult as lateral rein aids are imprecise and control over the poll is impossible.

Neck Ring

This playful form of a "bridle" is made of stiff lariat rope. It should loosely touch your horse's neck while you hold it in one or both hands. You apply precise pressure "impulses" to the neck, combined with weight and leg aids. Linda Tellington-Jones, founder of the Tellington Method®, sells one on her website (www.ttouch.com). Note: Never pull hard on a neck ring when it is in the horse's throat area.

Longeing Cavesson

The longeing cavesson is a snugly fitted bridle with a noseband that comes in different styles (Serreta, Cavecon, German, Pluvinel) and has several rings attached to it. It is used to longe and school young horses in hand. The longe line or a lead rope is attached to the ring in the middle of the noseband while reins or auxiliary reins are affixed to the rings on the sides.

It must be noted that the force effect of the longeing cavesson is significant. Depending on the material, it can be really heavy. Serreta and Cavecon types, for example, are reinforced with metal or are partly made of a U-shaped, padded piece of metal. The Serreta is even used without padding and sometimes with a serrated surface, which makes it extremely sharp.

Lindell Bitless Bridle

This bitless bridle developed by Linda Tellington-Jones is a side pull with a broad, usually padded nosepiece. It is very pleasant for horses and appropriate for use in beginner and children's lessons (www.ttouch.com).

LG Bridle™

This new invention, also called the "Happy Wheel," features a spoked wheel to which the cheekpieces, noseband, and reins are attached. Depending upon the configuration, it produces different effects, ranging from that of a side pull to a light or medium leverage effect. The reins act upon nose, chin, and poll after being diverted by the wheel. Lateral and vertical flexion can be attained so it can be used for advanced exercises.

Mechanical Hackamore

This bitless bridle has a padded noseband with a metal lever attached to each side. The levers come in different lengths. The length determines the leverage effect on the horse's nose and chin.

Please note: Long levers and slender nosebands can produce an extreme leverage effect on the horse's nasal bone! The metal lever is also easily twisted when only one rein exerts pull.

Meroth™ Bridle

The effect of the Meroth bridle is similar to the Bitless Bridle. It has leather cheekpieces that cross underneath the horse's chin, which in turn reduce the bridle's effect on the poll.

Rope Halter with Rings

Made of one piece of ¼-inch braided nylon rope, this knotted rope halter comes with two rings woven into the sides of the nosepiece so you can attach reins to it. You can also affix the reins to a loop underneath the chin, which turns it into a form of bosal. It is particularly useful during groundwork and lead rope training. Well-trained horses can also be ridden and longed with it.

Note: Since the rope this halter is made of is relatively thin, the effect can be very strong! The halter should be loosely fitted and its noseband should lie on the bony part of the nasal bone.

Side Pull

A side pull is a form of leather halter with reins attached at the sides. Your aids act upon the horse's head by way of the noseband, which comes in different materials: leather in various widths, padded or unpadded, lariat rope or braided rawhide. Rope and rawhide nosebands create uneven pressure, which makes them potentially harmful.

Final Words

With or without a bit, with or without a saddle, the foundation all riding is based on is the same: horses and people, being together.

Again and again, riders come to us completely astonished after their first experiences "without." They often say things like, "After a while, I didn't even think about the fact that I was riding without a 'proper bridle'!"

However, as we have said before, using one kind of bridle or another does not relieve you of the need to think for yourself, act responsibly, practice, acquire new skills, and further develop those you already have.

We believe that in the end, it does not matter at all what kind of equip-

ment a horse is wearing. If he can be controlled without reins and saddle, then riding with reins and saddle can always be a way of improving, refining, or specializing your riding. It's about the HOW instead of the WHAT.

We absolutely believe that you can ride your horse with a gentle bit if the horse is satisfied, relaxed, and active and the rider applies very subtle rein aids. But really, who wants to wear more clothes than outside temperatures require? Who goes for a hike in the mountains carrying extra pounds in their backpack? We can all agree that that would be nonsense!

The final decision is up to you.

Index

Page numbers in *italics* indicate illustrations.